AROUSING THE SPIRIT

Susan McCaslin

AROUSING THE SPIRIT

Provocative Writings

CopperHouse

Editor: Ellen Turnbull
Cover and interior design: Verena Velten
Book production: Margaret Kyle
Proofreader: Dianne Greenslade

SILVER
BNC CERTIFIED | BIBLIOGRAPHIC DATA 2011-12

CopperHouse is an imprint of Wood Lake Publishing, Inc. Wood Lake Publishing acknowledges the financial support of the Government of Canada, through the Book Publishing Industry Development Program (BPIDP) for its publishing activities. Wood Lake Publishing also acknowledges the financial support of the Province of British Columbia through the Book Publishing Tax Credit.

At Wood Lake Publishing, we practise what we publish, being guided by a concern for fairness, justice, and equal opportunity in all of our relationships with employees and customers. Wood Lake Publishing is committed to caring for the environment and all creation. Wood Lake Publishing recycles, reuses, and encourages readers to do the same. Resources are printed on 100% post-consumer recycled paper and more environmentally friendly groundwood papers (newsprint), whenever possible. A percentage of all profit is donated to charitable organizations.

Library and Archives Canada Cataloguing in Publication
McCaslin, Susan, 1947-
    Arousing the spirit : provocative writings / Susan McCaslin.

Issued also in an electronic format.
ISBN 978-1-55145-597-6
    1. Spiritual life. 2. Mysticism--Christianity. 3. Meditations.
I. Title.

BL624.2.M33 2011   204   C2011-904246-0

Copyright © 2011 Susan McCaslin
All rights are reserved. No part of this publication may be reproduced – except in the case of brief quotations embodied in critical articles and reviews – stored in an electronic retrieval system, or transmitted in any form or by any means, electronic, mechanical, photocopying, recording, or otherwise, without prior written permission of the publisher or copyright holder.

Published by CopperHouse
An imprint of Wood Lake Publishing Inc.
9590 Jim Bailey Road, Kelowna, BC, Canada, V4V 1R2
www.woodlakebooks.com
250.766.2778

Printing 10 9 8 7 6 5 4 3 2 1
Printed in Canada by
Houghton Boston

in memory of
Grace Jantzen (1948–2006):
feminist philosopher, theologian, friend

Gratitudes

To the following readers, whose thoughtful responses to the manuscript in its draft stages kept me focused:

Rev. Bruce Sanguin, Mark Haddock, Allan Briesmaster, James Clarke, Katerina Fretwell, J.S. Porter, Antoinette Voûte Roeder, Chris Dierkes, Celeste Snowber, Toni Pieroni, Sandy Shreve, Clélie Rich, Harold Rhenisch, and Penn Kemp.

I would like to thank Rev. Bruce Sanguin for inviting me to give the sermons (I call them Spirit Talks) that became the basis for this book.

To the treasured members of my memoir-writing group for meaningful feedback and support: Kate Braid, Heidi Greco, Joy Kogawa, and Marlene Schiwy.

To Music Minister Neil Weisensel, Minister of Pastoral Care Susan Dumoulin, and the entire congregation at Canadian Memorial United Church for encouraging me to first present some of the chapters from this book within the context of liturgy.

To Ellen Turnbull, my insightful, indefatigable, and intuitive editor at Wood Lake Publishing for seeing the potential in my manuscript from the start and helping me make it sing.

Finally, to my husband Mark Haddock, environmental activist, for his unfailing support, and for our 34-year conversation about all matters spiritual.

Contents

Preface 10
Chapter 1: The Problem with Perfect 17
Chapter 2: Jester Jesus 35
Chapter 3: Transforming the Shadow 49
Chapter 4: The Paradise Ear 65
Chapter 5: Countering War with Wonder 83
Chapter 6: Rapturous Ravishments 99
Chapter 7: The Palace of Presence 119
Chapter 8: A Warless World 133
Chapter 9: Blessed 147
Chapter 10: Peaceful Resisters 163
Chapter 11: Fire on Fire 177
Chapter 12: Opening to Mystery 191
Chapter 13: I Am 207
Chapter 14: Re-visioning Revelation 223
Acknowledgements 240

Preface

I am a poet who was roused, awakened, by what I called God when I was about seven years old. The verb "to rouse" was used originally to describe "hawks shaking the feathers of the body," a rather appropriate image for a sense of spiritual excitation and enthrallment. Later the word came to mean simply "to stir up, provoke to activity."[1]

In many sacred traditions spiritual arousal or awakening lies at the very heart of things. Empathy and compassion must be awakened in us before we can embody them in our lives.

My early spiritual concepts were conditioned by my Presbyterian upbringing, but somehow the mystical side of religion, the sense of direct experience of the divine, of the interior Christ, was what really mattered. From early childhood I had a sense of the divine as a loving, compassionate presence within me, beyond me, and present in everything else, though I wouldn't have articulated my intuitions in this way. Later, in high school, I was stirred up by the God of Poetry, or, you could say, the God of Poetry began to awaken in me.

This mystical, mysterious God transcended gender and lay in a realm beyond explanation, something like a Poem making itself new in each instant. Hans Christian Anderson, the Bible, and the poetry of Robert Louis Stevenson and Tennyson first provided me with continuing entrances into enchantment. Whether experienced through the pulse of writing, meditation, or daily life, an intense longing to awaken and be awakened by Spirit never completely left.

Spirit for me is that in each of us that wants (needs) to make meaning and purpose out of the particularities of our everyday lives. For me as a literary person and as a poet, this quest has everything to do with language, the interplay between words and silence. In both my life and in my writing, Spirit mysteriously appears, disappears, and reappears. There are times when I think the original intensity has abandoned me, only to discover it has gone underground like a lustrous stream that breaks to the surface from hidden depths.

In putting together this book of writings on various aspects of Spirit's erotic, activating powers, I drew on some of my public talks, essays, and new pieces of writing. Interspersed among the prose pieces are short poems that stand as angelic guardians at the gates of the chapters – prayers of opening to Spirit. Though the subject matter may at first seem diverse, the book hangs on a single thread: the states and stages of mystical awakening.

The word arousal, of course, can have both sexual and spiritual connotations. Spirit arouses us like a lover arouses his or her beloved. And we arouse or awaken Spirit by our creativity and openness to transformation. In the Song of Songs, the two speakers (the exotic Shulamite or dark maiden and her elusive lover, King Solomon), engage in mutual acts of arousal. He awakens her; she awakens him. This sacred text works splendidly at both the literal and symbolic levels, for it is about both physical and spiritual union:

> I adjure you, O daughters of Jerusalem, by the gazelles or the wild does: do not stir up or awaken [arouse] love until it is ready.
> ~ *SONG OF SONGS, 3:5*

Poet-songwriter Leonard Cohen writes about a similar reversal of roles between lover and beloved in "You Have Loved Enough."

> And when the hunger for your touch
> Rises from the hunger,
> You whisper, "You have loved enough,
> Now let me be the Lover."[2]

Cohen here plays with the same fusion of secular and spiritual meanings. God the lover tells the soul or individual it is time to let Spirit take over and take the lead in lovemaking. Love is a dance in which first one lover then the other leads. Only when we in our small selfhoods are exhausted with trying to love our own way can we let go enough to let the divine take over and love us fully and completely.

My sense of life as a mystical dance took deeper root when at the age of twenty-two I first came to British Columbia from the United States to do graduate work at Simon Fraser University. Shortly after crossing the border with my draft-resisting boyfriend in 1969, I met a living Christian mystic, Olga Park. I make references to Olga's teaching and insights in several of these chapters.

Olga generously shared with me her own practice of contemplative prayer and her lifetime of mystical experiences. Her practice was something like the ancient Christian meditative practice now called centring prayer or contemplative prayer, whereby one opens to the silences deep within. When I married my British Columbian-born husband in 1979, he joined me in this contemplative practice. So my childhood spiritual sensitivity, which I had to some extent abandoned during university, was allowed to reawaken and evolve.

The writings in this book reflect my central passions over a lifetime: mysticism (or the direct experience of the sacred) and its place in everyday life; peacemaking and justice; the importance of the non-canonical Gospels like the Gospel of Thomas; the place of the miraculous in contemporary liberal theology; the relation of spirituality and sexuality; and the significance of Jesus of Nazareth once divested of outworn theology and his sappy Hollywood persona.

I have attempted to lift the biblical stories and sayings out of a tribal context and reveal their universal meaning as wisdom teaching. Some of the chapters reflect my commitment to inter-spirituality – the profound interconnections among not only the various religions and spiritual traditions, but among the human and other-than-human species and life forms on our fragile and beautiful planet.

I hope you will treat these pieces like meditations sprung from the oral tradition. Feel free to skip around. Read the book from back to front if you like. It is not just for the religious, or for Christians, but also for anyone who is alienated from religion but interested in spirituality. It's also for those who consider themselves agnostics (those who accept a state of unknowing) but wish to remain open to more than materialist explanations of life. It is even for atheists who can't accept a theistic God who manipulates things from outside on behalf of "his chosen ones" or tribe of "true believers."

Writing this book has helped me rediscover the depths of my own Christian heritage with a mind and heart open to the world's great mystical traditions. In the end, what we do and how we act in the world is more significant than what we profess to believe or the various doctrines and ideologies we espouse.

May these speculative probings become for you little energy fields opening to the greater, cosmic playfields of joy, peace, and wholeness.

---

1 Online etymology dictionary: http://www.etymonline.com/index.php?term=rouse
2 Leonard Cohen, *Ten New Songs*, Sony Recordings, 2001.

Chapter One

The Problem with Perfect

But I say to you, Love your enemies and pray for those who persecute you, so that you may be children of your Father in heaven; for he makes his sun rise on the evil and on the good, and sends rain on the righteous and on the unrighteous...Be perfect, therefore, as your heavenly Father is perfect.

~ MATTHEW 5:44–48

Holy One,
be in us an awakening and a movement.

Silent One,
be in us a stillness and a rest.

Speaking One,
be in us a spiraling song.

Whole One,
be in us a mending wall.

Fullness,
be in us a brimming cup.

Ripening One,
be in us a pomegranate's praise.

Emptied One,
be in us a cup poured out.

Ever New One,
draw from us more surprises.

Luminous One,
be in our flaws an aperture of light

that we may be whole as you are whole,
that we may be ripe as you are ripe,

that we may be always within you
as you are within us,

beloved Partner and Friend.

When I was a girl I tended to take on a lot of household responsibility and be overly conscientious at school. Some people called me Little Miss Perfect. I knew at the time I was far from perfect, especially in the sense of "flawless," so this label confused me and didn't make me feel any better about myself.

When we say someone is perfect, we often mean that they approximate an ideal we all know no one can really emulate. This kind of perfectionism is tied to the myth of the infinite perfectibility of the material world and of our status within it through individual effort. It is at the root of a deep malaise in Western culture.

Modern perfectionism and the accompanying sense of never measuring up often lead to self-criticism. After a little research, I found that it was not until 1656 that the word was used in the theological sense as "the notion that moral perfection may be attained in earthly existence." And it was not until 1934 that "perfectionist" was used to indicate "one only satisfied with the highest standards."

Perfectionism in our culture affects our youth in dire ways. Young girls, and increasingly boys, ingest the images of unhealthy thinness or extreme buffness that inundate them in the media and sometimes find themselves struggling with anorexia and "anorexia athletica." Moms and dads often become workaholics in the quest for perfect careers, communicating with each other mostly through email. Many of us, despite our regimented lifestyles, are burdened with a sense of always missing the mark, which is itself an older Greek definition of sin or error.[1] We are constantly face to face with entropy, sagging bellies, the sense that things are running down, time is running out, and that despite all our best efforts, as Bob Dylan puts it, "everything is broken." We come to believe that to be happy we need a better face, body, car, or house, and are then urged by advertising to purchase that gadget or lifestyle that will grant us happiness. Advertisers study how to play on this desire for self-improvement and on our endless dissatisfaction with our imperfect selves.

It's easy to see how the quest for perfectionism is futile in the realm of material things, but what about in art, athletics, and morality – areas where perfectionism seems appropriate? If we don't strive for excellence, would we create great works of art? Would Michelangelo have lain on his back for years inscribing breathlessness into the hand of Adam on the Sistine ceiling? Or did he lie stretched there for so long because he was totally in love with the beauty that inspired him? Doesn't the culture benefit from artists who are somewhat obsessive-compulsive? And don't Olympic athletes strive to transcend the limits of the body for excellence in the sport?

A desire to supersede limits is a part of the human spirit; yet there is a distinction between pushing the boundaries for the love of the art or sport, and pushing for fame, approval, and applause. Truly great artists and athletes seldom lose sight of the joy of creation or the activity's intrinsic pleasure. If this element of joy is eradicated, both art and sport lose their heart.

Jesus and Perfection

In the passage from Matthew at the beginning of this chapter, Jesus says, "Be perfect, therefore, as your heavenly Father is perfect." Some might take Jesus' words to (wrongly) mean that perfection is a matter of gritting your moral teeth and "loving" a person who let you down or injured you so that God can heap blessings on your head for going so against your natural impulse to feel anger. However, in New Testament Greek, the term "perfect" here is *teleios,* meaning "unblemished, complete, finished, full-grown." But how can we hear Jesus' encouragement as anything but an insistence on the impossible?

The word perfection has many rich connotations throughout the Bible. Though the New Testament was written in Greek, Jesus used Aramaic, where the word for perfect (*gmar*) is closer to "ripe," "fully flavoured," or "fully flowered."[2] Perfection involves a fulfillment of the potential a thing has within itself all along from the seed state. In Latin, the word means "completely formed or performed," and the verb "to perfect" means "to bring to full development." The Hebrew word for perfect, *taman*, also means something close to "mature," "whole," "complete." In these older contexts, perfection is a dynamic process to which we surrender. We know we can't bring about this maturity by ourselves, but have to be part of what constantly re-creates itself and moves toward balance and wholeness. Perfection could be redefined, then, as opening to the flow of the whole – which is the flow of divine love.

Let's return, then, to what Jesus might have had in mind when he said to his disciples that they needed to love their enemies. God, who loves perfectly, sees "the enemy" as part of the field of awareness one calls oneself. Let's try translating the phrase this way: "Be whole, be part of a loving motion toward completeness." Or "Be in the flowing light of the Godhead," or "Look at things from a perspective that intuits how all things are interconnected." If we redefine the term this way, then love of the enemy might begin to issue from the heart without so much moral strain, and the enemy we are called to love could be ourselves.

Imagine a shift of consciousness in which we stop seeing the world in terms of self and other, me and you, them and us. If this perception could be sustained, then loving the enemy might not be a matter of just being nice to someone nasty. Jesus nudges his disciples to assume the viewpoint of a loving, all-compassionate parent. Such an act of identification with universal compassion is not impossible if in our deepest interiors we dwell in God and God dwells in us. Jesus' statement, then, is that of a mystic, or one who has experienced directly this sort of oneness and begun to live out of it in a constant way.

Embracing the Imperfect

When we think of the legacy of the mystics, we hear much of an ascent through stages of mystical perfection to ultimate unity, fulfillment, or realization. In the East, the quest for unified being has been called enlightenment. Such traditions of "the perfect" can be useful today, but they must be re-contextualized.

Perhaps the kind of perfectionism that spoils both art and life is that which rejects the transitory and limited. Great artists know that, as Wallace Stevens states, "the imperfect is our paradise." Leonard Cohen gets it right when he sings, "There is a crack in everything; that's how the light gets in." In fact, however much we affirm what

Stevens calls the "blessed rage for order," the universe as we know it is not a neat and tidy place.

Greatness involves giving over our little orderings in the grand Chaos to an order beyond our present comprehension. We are opened to a needful disturbance. In other words, God's kitchen is a fecund mess that ends in a festive banquet. The vastness of star-strewn space suggests a cosmic order, but not a rigid, fathomable one. This is why poets, artists, city planners, architects, and ecologists feel a part of something larger than their original intent. In the creative process, plots and plans may go askew as newness invades. Perhaps heaven is not a topiary garden but a rain forest with falling trees, rotting nurse logs, and the mysterious activity of microbes.

Perfectionism resists this fertile chaos out of fear: it wants to evade the essential breaking open. The ego likes to keep to the past, to safe strategies that have worked before, while Spirit says, "Behold, I destroy your blunders and pasty efforts and blow them to smithereens to make all things new."

To enter such a process of *kenosis* or letting go requires courage, because one never knows what will have to be sacrificed. Sometimes what a writer thinks are the finest bits have to go. Sometimes they seem like clearings of the throat that must be resigned to the waste bin. Perhaps those Tibetan monks who make sand mandalas are closer to the truth of art than those who are too much focused on product. After weeks of painstaking labour, they consign the work of their hands to water.

Letting Go into the General Dance

Following the call to perfection requires some striving. It also requires letting go. With this in mind, there are common usages of the word perfect that seem perfectly fitting. A dog lolling on a lawn, for instance, is perfect because she is completely at one with the moment and is not being anything other than herself. The birds of the air and the lilies of the field are perfect, as Jesus observed, because they "toil not neither do they spin." They naturally let life ripple through and complete them. When the French say a meal is *parfait,* they mean it is completely satisfying and right. And when the mystics speak of "the ladder of perfection," or "the scale of perfection," they have in mind an ascending evolutionary spiral through various phases of consciousness, not the attainment of a static perfection.

Perhaps another way of putting it is that if you want to enter the cosmic dance where all is in the process of increasing the amount of love in the universe, anywhere you are along the way can be right and in harmony. Rejecting perfectionism, as opposed to perfection, doesn't mean that there are no deeper levels of maturity in the spiritual life.

It is helpful to look at Jesus as one who, like us, was birthed to oneness through a process of transformation. To make Jesus of Nazareth into the flawless only Son of God diminishes him. In fact, the belief that Jesus was the perfect lamb who died for our sins is wrongheaded because it denies the love and compassion of God and our direct access to the fountains of mercy.

Perfection and Atonement

The doctrine of atonement implies that God cannot forgive humans except through a blood sacrifice. The harmful notion of Christian perfectionism I have been describing is deeply rooted in this doctrine (developed in the 11th century by Bishop Anselm) of Jesus as the perfect sacrifice.[3] Atonement doctrine returns us to the primitive image of a God who regresses to human sacrifice, where the purity of the victim is directly connected with the efficacy of the sacrifice.

Though some might say we can relax into our imperfection because Jesus has done everything for us on the cross, the notion of God requiring a perfect sacrifice complicates the problem. If Jesus' perfection rests on his union with God, then why would a loving God construct a universe that requires him to sacrifice this union with his only son in order to forgive humanity? The teaching of Jesus in The Lord's Prayer, on the contrary, is clearly that we need to forgive as we are forgiven, and that God's compassion and love are boundless and unconditional.

The Christian tradition has had an irrational ambiguity around perfectionism: imitate Christ, try to be perfect like him, but don't try too hard because you can never be like him. In fact, being imperfect is good news because the perfect like Jesus are torn to pieces anyway. In our own culture, a similar phenomenon is evident in the public's adulation of film stars. We admire them for their perfect bodies, clothes, lifestyles, and charisma, but we also love to tear them down.

Similarly in the Middle Ages, the populace admired the spiritual austerities of the saints, who often wished to emulate in their bodies the suffering of Christ. When my young daughter was travelling in Italy, she stopped in Siena to visit the church of St. Catherine of Siena. Though impressed with the saint's mystical legacy, the image of her tiny skull, no bigger than a child's because of years of extreme fasting, was disturbing. I visited this church later and wrote of my daughter's impression, using the classical Greek figure of the young goddess Persephone, queen of the underworld, to represent the young women inducted into our culture's mythos of perfectionism.

Persephone Stands Stalled Before the Shrine of Catherine of Siena

the instruments of self-flagellation, the account
of her final self-starvation.

Stench of sanctity appalls:
embalmed skull, relic of her diminution,

no larger than a three-year-old child's.

"Holy Anorexic," they named you,
wizened, wiser now?

And Holy you are and were and are to be
in word and text,

but unholy, unholy the culture
that urged this self-effacement,

*abasement, erasure of flesh
your sole path to purity.*

*You who were clean and fresh
as first narcissus in a field,*

*not vain, but veined
with green causeways of our mother,*

*stem and branch of our mutual source,
Mater Gaia, she who emerged from Chaos*

overturning sleep to make us well.[4]

Evolutionary Ascent to Wholeness

I'd like to add one last thought about the movement toward what has been called our "perfecting in the glory." Unlike dogs and birds that have not so radically separated themselves from the ground of being, humans need to be intentional about the pursuit of wholeness.

Anyone who enters seriously on a spiritual path comes to realize that there are various stages of development along the way. One of the first things the Dalai Lama asked contemplative monk Thomas Merton was something like, "What sort of program for ascent or advancement through various stages of consciousness do you pursue in your Christian monastic orders?" Jesus encouraged the practice of entering into one's closet (the deep interiority). He recommended regular and frequent times of accessing divine presence through practices like prayer and contemplation.

In mystical ascent, the top of the mountain isn't the only perfect place to be: there is also beauty and rightness along the whole of the path. When Jesus tells a certain rich young ruler that if he wants to be perfect and inherit *eternal* or timeless consciousness he needs to give away everything he has and follow him (Jesus), something much more than our modern perfectionism is at stake.

In the end, what is needed is a raising of consciousness in which body, mind, emotions, and spirit are in balance with the great Spirit that moves the sun and the stars. Out of this global consciousness may issue social justice and equality – the kingdom of heaven on earth. This process does not require perfectionism in the modern sense, but a mindful spiritual practice in conjunction with a simple opening of the heart to greater oneness with the hidden wholeness that already lies deep within each of us.

---

1   Lehman Strauss, *The Doctrine of Sin.* http://bible.org/article/doctrine-sin

2   Neil Douglas-Klotz, *The Hidden Gospel: Decoding the Spiritual Message of the Aramaic Jesus* (Wheaton, Il.: The Theosophical Publishing House, 1999), 129.

3   Marcus J. Borg, *Jesus: Uncovering the Life, Teachings, and Relevance of a Religious Community* (NY: HarperSanFrancisco, 1989), 268.

4   Susan McCaslin, *Persephone Tours the Underground* (Vancouver, BC: Alfred Gustav Press, 2009), 9. See also *Demeter Goes Skydiving* (Edmonton, Alberta: University of Alberta Press, 2011).

Chapter Two

Jester Jesus

For God's foolishness is wiser than human wisdom.
　　　　　　　　　~ 1 CORINTHIANS 1:25

If a [wo]man would persist in [her] his folly, [s]he would become wise.
　　　　　　　　　~ WILLIAM BLAKE

Dear Clown of God,

Jesus of jests and holy foolery,
spin us on the wheel of your wit
till we fall on the floor laughing
at the deep simplicity of it all.

Teach us to dance like David,
to fling off our heavy suits like Francis,
tease the Caesars of this world
till they fall earthward like children.

Let's all dine together
at the madcap feast of fools,
playing hide and seek
with our too-certain identities.

*Be in us crazy wisdom,
smarter than the savvy heads
of corporations. Incorporate us
into the body electric.*

*Tickle our fancy, till we fancy
joys beyond materialism.
Make us laugh into tears
and weep into the glory of now.*

The portrayal of Jesus in much visual art, film, and the culture at large is that of someone almost entirely lacking in a sense of humour. He has appeared as an ethereal guy in a white robe and sandals pontificating solemnly in high-flown King James English, walking on water or floating about three inches off the ground. In the old Hollywood films, Jesus comes across as someone totally unreal, beyond the common humanity.

His air of transcendence is partly due to the belief that the earthy Rabbi Jesus was God in the flesh. Though the early Christian communities saw their teacher as godly in spirit, not all early Christians equated Jesus with God. The doctrines of the Trinity and the Incarnation were not part of Jesus' original teachings about himself, but emerged slowly and were refined as church teaching around the time of the Council of Nicaea in the fourth century.

Jesus' lack of humour in these portrayals is an enormous loss, since humour is a quality that most of us desire in a teacher, friend, or mate. When I was hoping to meet my life's companion, I put a good sense of humour high on my wish list. For without the ability to laugh at oneself or see the comic in a situation, a person comes off as rigid or inauthentic. Without laughter, life is pretty sterile and boring.

However, a close reading of the Gospels reveals Jesus not only as a wisdom teacher and activist but as a young rabbi with an infectious, ironic, daring, irresistible sense of humour. This must have been one of the things that drew large crowds to him.

Transformative Trickster

About a decade ago, I had a brief conversation with a poet acquaintance of mine about the figure of Jesus. My friend suggested he had no real interest in Christianity because it lacked a trickster figure like the ones in the aboriginal cultures, a dynamo like Raven or Coyote. Tricksters in world mythologies dwell at the margins of society between one plane of being and another. They are threshold-dwellers, quixotic, unpredictable, and sometimes perceived as "bad" or outside the bounds of conventional morality. Tricksters often break the rules and upset normalcy, but end up ushering in an element of creative transformation.

All these years later, it occurs to me that Jesus is indeed one of the great trickster figures in both myth and history – playful, wise, and hard to pin down. Like most tricksters, he has a propensity to suddenly disappear and reappear. He jests with and teases his disciples. You think he's dead and he pops up alive. In short, he's fascinating, smart, edgy, and a transformer.

In the Gospels, Jesus' humour isn't innocuous. He gets

outright enraged at injustice, cruelty, power-mongering, and greed. Much of his ironic wit is directed at the Pharisees, though I suspect in reality much more of it targeted the occupying Romans who were oppressing the poor and threatening local subversive Jewish movements. Yet whether in response to the Romans or to the hierarchy of the temple system, Jesus had no truck with hypocrisy.

Jesus makes a sharp comment about how the Pharisees "strain at gnats and swallow camels" (Matthew 23:24). Scholar William Phipps points out that this saying would have been even more powerful in Jesus' native Aramaic due to the word play on gnat *(kalma)* and camel *(gamla)*.[1] In an unsuccessful attempt to strain a tiny gnat out from his wine glass to make it ritually pure, a scrupulous Pharisee accidentally swallows a camel instead. The absurdity of the image adds weight to Jesus' suggestion that when it comes to spirituality we tend to focus on the trivial, missing faults that are potentially much more damaging.

Jesus' well-known anecdotes and sayings are so overlaid with pious sentimentality and custom that we don't see how radical he truly was. If we look more deeply, and overcome anesthetization by familiarity, the laughter of Jesus suddenly hits us. Let me give you a few examples.

Think about his saying about missing the log in our own eye while trying to pick the speck out of someone else's. Now imagine this literally. The hyperbole is as potent as ever: "Hey, big guy, let me help you with that dust particle." Meanwhile the Douglas fir plank looming from our own eye goes unnoticed and dangerously stabs the air.

I heard the story of Jesus calling the disciples Peter and Andrew from their fishing nets and promising to make them fishers of human beings (Matthew 4:19) over and over in Sunday school, where the gravity of being called to serve God was impressed on me. When I read it now, it's as if Jesus is saying: "Hey dudes, forget the small fry; why not try catching a few people in those nets?" It's a jest, a dare, a challenge.

Like Rabbi Hillel of Jesus' own time with his wise and witty maxims, and the later Hasidic masters of the Middle Ages, Jesus creates stories with unexpected twists and turns. In one parable Jesus seems to rationalize a situation where employees who come on board for a job at the end of the day get paid the same as those who started at the crack of dawn (Matthew 20:1–16). In a trickster-like way, he overturns his audience's conventional expectations of fairness. We are made to realize God isn't always "fair" by human standards. Jesus notes that disasters fall on the "just and unjust alike." He isn't for those who like a morally tidy universe or a sense that everything works out equitably this side of eternity. He loves paradoxes, conundrums, and apparent contradictions, like the idea of the meek inheriting the earth or the poor being the happiest. Go figure!

In a series of three parables about lost things found, Jesus moves from the story of the lost sheep, to the story of the lost coin, and then caps the trilogy with the story of the prodigal or lost son (Luke 15:1–32). Since in all three parables the one who seeks the lost thing or person symbolizes God, what's surprising here is that Jesus sandwiches a story of a woman down on her hands and knees looking for a lost coin between the other two. Quite suddenly, the Jewish audience is asked to imagine God as a woman rummaging around on the kitchen floor. This image has radical implications in a patriarchal society.

Jesus the teaser has a jaunty, rough-and-tumble way of joking with his disciples, giving them nicknames like Sons of Thunder for the rather conventional James and John, and the Rock for unstable Peter. His trickster's trick is to give someone a nickname that is the exact opposite of what that person most seems to represent. The teasing of Peter is less a chiding than a sly wink at both his friend's foibles and his hidden potential to be rock solid.

Another episode of gentle teasing occurs at the end of John where the risen Jesus tells the chastened Peter three times to "feed my sheep." Here Jesus echoes deliberately the three times Peter insisted to a servant girl on the night before the crucifixion that he didn't know Jesus. Some have taken this to be a gentle admonition on Jesus' part, a sort of shaming of Peter while forgiving him at the same time. I see it as more of a joke. The teacher is having a bit of fun, but his tone tells Peter there's no judgment, just awareness of their common humanity.

Tricksters are cunning and won't be put into boxes. We find Jester Jesus getting out of a pickle by turning the question back on the questioner who is trying to entrap him into an incriminating statement: "Whose head is this [on this coin]?...Give to the emperor the things that are the emperor's, and to God the things that are God's." (Mark 12:16–17). Jesus pulls us in and makes us question our beliefs. *Well, what does actually belong to the emperor? What does belong to God?*

Tricksters don't hand out simple answers. They force us to come up with a response and solve the enigma ourselves. "Who do you say that I am?" How you see me says more about you than it does about me, Jesus implies. Like Socrates, Jesus uses irony to expose the hidden motives of his opponents.

We have had more than 2000 years of the sorrowful Jesus in art and film, but not heard much about the joyful Jesus. Yet the "man of sorrows acquainted with grief" and the jokester Jesus are equally important and represent two poles of a complex consciousness. The weeping and the laughter of Jesus need to be put together to make a complete picture.

In the Coptic *Apocalypse of Peter* (200–250 BCE), for

instance, Jesus is depicted laughing above the cross, having transcended suffering even at the moment of his most intense suffering. Jesus explains this image to Peter:

> He whom you saw on the tree, glad and laughing, this is the living Jesus. But this one into whose hands and feet they drive the nails is his fleshly part, which is the substitute being put to shame, the one who came into being in his likeness.[2]

The traditional reading of this text is that Jesus didn't actually die on the cross (a belief called Docetism held by some of the early Gnostics). While I don't happen to agree with this view, I ask myself what happens if we read this scene symbolically. I think the passage means Jesus' physical body died on the cross, but his soul and spirit ultimately transcended the ordeal.

In another text we are told that Jesus danced with his disciples on the night before his crucifixion. This account in *The Gnostic Acts of John* (second century) called *The Round Dance of the Cross* may have been the basis for the folk song *Lord of the Dance*.[3] And in the Gospel of Matthew there is the moment when Jesus and his disciples sing a hymn as they head out to Gethsemane (Matthew 26:30). All this suggests that Jesus' *joie de vivre* and energy couldn't be destroyed, even when he was facing torture and death.

Cosmic Clown

In the context of seeing Jesus as a man of mirth, I'd like to share with you a story about an experience I had in 1992 where Jesus appeared to me precisely as a fool, a cosmic clown of God. At the time, I was troubled about an unresolved illness. During the waiting period for the results of various medical tests, while praying at my home prayer table, I slipped briefly into a vision state where the following scenario played itself out. I wrote in my journal at the time:

> Jesus appears on the stage (actually wearing a white robe and sandals) and asks me to lay out my troubles. From my seat in the audience, I begin to verbalize them, one at a time, while he listens patiently. Each fear rolls off my tongue in the form of an enormous metallic block shaped like a cube. Every block is larger and heavier than the one before. There are seven in all. When I reach the last and weightiest, he says, "That one is fear itself." Then he adds, "All you have to do now is push them a little way toward me." So I come up on the stage, and with great effort, nudge each block only a few inches towards him. When I am done, he praises, "Excellent!" then proceeds to carry the blocks offstage one at a time, the lightest

first. For me they had felt like lead, but for him they seem feather-light. When he hoists the final and weightiest one, he laughs, sailing it high over his head, twirling it on his forefinger like a juggler or clown in a circus. He exits stage left and disappears behind the curtain. Then, as if having an afterthought, he pokes out his head from behind the drapery and winks, "Don't worry, I'm blowing them all to dust."

The vision dismantled my fears, and a month later all the tests came back negative. It also replaced my serious notion of a "gentle Jesus meek and mild" with a cosmic trickster full of surprises.

For too long Christianity has been presented as a sober, sombre, serious business, such as my Presbyterian ancestors believed. Yet in the wisdom literature of the First Testament, the universe unfolds as a cosmic play or drama. In Proverbs 8, Sophia or Holy Wisdom plays before her partner, the Holy One. She is at once his complementary opposite and the feminine presence of God from the foundation of the world. If God(dess) plays, then to participate in Her we too are called to play, to dance, to experience heart-pounding, deep, belly-laughing joy. We are invited to join the cosmic dance, romping and tumbling like puppies or children absorbed in a game.

Why is laughter so important? Laughter softens us and makes us whole. To laugh is to take our ego-bound selves a lot less seriously. Laughter deflates our pretenses and helps us get real. It spontaneously unifies us with the divine flow of things. Laugher is an expression of the freedom to be and to explore, to break with conventional behaviour and create new possibilities. It turns the world around and helps us see from other angles. Or maybe it turns us around. Wisdom, as Shakespeare knew when he linked King Lear with his faithful fool, is foolery. Holy foolery.

---

1 William E. Phipps, *The Wit and Wisdom of Rabbi Jesus* (Louisville, Kentucky: Westminster/John Knox Press, 1993), 87.

2 http://theunjustmedia.com/Islamic%20Perspectives/The%20Crucifixion%20of%20Jesus.htm

3 http://www.gnosis.org/library/actjohn.htm

Chapter Three

Transforming the Shadow

Jesus, full of the Holy Spirit, returned from the Jordan and was led by the Spirit in the wilderness, where for forty days he was tempted by the devil. He ate nothing at all during those days, and when they were over, he was famished. The devil said to him, "If you are the Son of God, command this stone to become a loaf of bread." Jesus answered him, "It is written, 'One does not live by bread alone.'"

~ LUKE 4:1–4

Each man is in his Spectre's power
Until the arrival of that hour
When his Humanity awake
And cast his Spectre into the Lake.

~ WILLIAM BLAKE (NOTEBOOKS)

Healer and Transformer,

Be in our desert, a thousand underground fountains.

Be in our wrestling, a voice praising.
Widen our dreams, expand our texts.

Help us transform our hampering shadows
that cling and whisper, "Look at me,"

so we can praise the violet in its sheltered opening,
the cedar in its fanfare of expanding rings.

Grant us the courage to face our shadow
when selfhood crafts a fixed mask

*and fear flaunts its iron citadels.
Open to us your jubilant Jerusalems.*

*Feed us the Bread of Life
as you would a small child,*

*and grant us the chance to serve
what flares in Love's trembling web.*

If we actually enumerated our guilt-thoughts in a single day, I think most of us would be shocked. The other day I was considering how often I feel guilty or second-guess myself. An object goes missing in the house, and because I tend to be the one in my family to tidy and put things away I immediately blame myself for throwing it out or misplacing it. I tell a friend she can't come over because I need some time alone in which to write, but beat up on myself for being inhospitable and anti-social. In the name of being helpful and to maintain a bit of control I do things for my daughter that she can better do for herself, then feel guilty for having done them.

In the world of Jungian psychology, these (mostly unacknowledged) parts of ourselves full of fear, desire for control, and self-loathing that we sometimes project on others are called the shadow. The shadow is a composite of all those qualities, urges, feelings, thoughts, and ways of being that we associate with "badness" and therefore deny. This negative energy leaks out unconsciously and keeps us from being in alignment with self, others, and Spirit.

In all the great religious traditions, the mystics, saints, and wisdom teachers *struggled* greatly with, and transformed, their shadows. So when I was rereading the familiar narrative of Jesus' temptation in the desert (Luke 4:1–12), I wondered about Jesus' shadow.

When my theology was much more traditional than it is today, I would have thought such a query about Jesus almost blasphemous. I considered Jesus "fully human and fully divine." If Jesus was divine, as many traditionalists assume, he wouldn't have had much of a shadow. Now it seems to me that to remove any real conflict from the temptation story is to diminish Jesus. In fact, what makes Jesus great is that he struggled with his shadow, met it face to face, and transformed it.

In Luke's narrative, Satan represents that part of human consciousness identified with the greedy, self-centred, power-hungry aspect of the ego when it attempts to appropriate to itself the whole. The question is whether the part will serve the whole, or try to coerce the whole into serving the part. My suspicion is that Jesus as a young man knew he had charisma, special healing abilities, and a unique mission related to his vision of God's kingdom. Yet attending these qualities could have been a nagging fear that he was in it for himself, or that a part of him had the potential to become attracted to power or caught up in using the ends to justify the means.

The Devil's voice represents the self-contradictory one in all of us that simultaneously undermines our confidence while puffing us up. Out of one side of the mouth it taunts, "Who do you think you are, big shot?" With the other it flatters, "Okay, you are exceptional. You can do good things and yet serve your needs for self-aggrandizement at the same time. Go ahead, turn the stones into bread; take up the leadership of a movement; consider yourself specially protected." By listening to either or both of these false voices we place the ego or small self and its needs first: "If you, then, will worship me, the kingdoms of this world will all be yours."

The truth is exactly the reverse; if one puts the self or ego first, the world gained is not the kingdom of heaven but a limited kingdom of one's own making that is sure to collapse. Happily, the story tells us that Jesus did his inner work with power and the potential for its abuse.

On another occasion, Jesus says to Peter, "Get behind me, Satan." He doesn't say, "Get out of here, Satan." Jesus knows that the egoic self is a construction that is an important part of himself, so he embraces it rather than running from it. He does not reject the constructed selfhood entirely, but does not allow it to lead or to determine his actions.

Strangely enough, Jesus goes on to perform in new contexts the apparently rejected, miraculous feats Satan tempted him with. After facing down his inner demons, Jesus comes to use his power authentically. He doesn't shy away from being a leader. He lets the crowds follow him, acknowledges his role as teacher, prophet and even Messiah (in at least some of the scriptures), and continually refuses to use the power that flows through him for himself alone. Service becomes his signature. At the wedding in Cana (John 2:1–11), he transforms water into wine not for himself but for the celebration of the kingdom. In the various accounts of the feeding of the five-thousand (Matthew 14, Luke 9, Mark 6, and John 6) he multiplies substance to feed the crowds. And his healings, of course, are both manifestations of the power of God and acts of love and compassion.

Some scientists and theologians suggest that what we designate as matter and what we call spirit could be one substance in various phases of transformation and metamorphosis. Einstein argued for a time and space continuum. Stones over infinite time may indeed become bread, and bread stones; the molecules of our bodies may become parts of stars and vice versa. So it is not the act of transformation itself that is problematic. The desire to manipulate it in our own rather than cosmic timing, to use it for ourselves rather than for the health and life of the whole is the problem. It is the inappropriate use of power that needs to be renounced.

Furthermore, this principle of interconnection that Jesus so often highlights in his wisdom sayings suggests that everything affects everything else. If this is so, then it is wisest to serve the whole because we are a part encompassed by that whole and the wholeness dwells in us.

In a sense, serving the larger whole rather than the broken shadow is a paradigm for ecological wellness: "In so far as you do it to one of the least of these, you do it to me."

Yet Jesus did not live by the wisdom that flowed through him without struggle. In the Gospel of Mark, for instance, a gentile woman has to get Jesus' attention with an ironic quip about how "even the dogs under the table eat of the children's crumbs" before Jesus is willing to heal her ailing daughter. Bruce Sanguin of Canadian Memorial United Church suggests this particular incident reveals a moment when Jesus evolves from ethnocentric to universal in his capacity for love.[1]

In the end, Jesus opens himself to God's power, performs the miracles, and walks as a divine child of Sophia-Wisdom. Yet it is because he has acknowledged his shadow and set it behind him that he becomes the Christ.

After Jesus enters the wilderness or wild places of his own psyche, we see the emergence of a person who consistently opts for service, humility, and non-violence. He teaches a mysterious kingdom that slowly emerges in the outer world if first nurtured and birthed in the heart – a kingdom of peace and love in which no one dominates another and all are servants. He rides into Jerusalem, but chooses a lowly donkey on which to ride. He speaks as one who has had direct experience of the Holy One, and reveals God as a unifying power of unconditional love, compassion, and mercy that his disciples may enact by washing each other's feet. He never reneges on the power that flows through him, especially when asserting it against the corruption of worldly systems, though doing so results in his crucifixion.

Jesus struggles from moment to moment with the issues raised in the archetypal event of the temptation, but the overall shape of his life and teachings shows he surrendered everything to a higher good. He was able to integrate his shadow because his concept and experience of God was of a love so powerful it could accept him, shadow and all. Therefore, he was not crippled by his doubts and fears, but open to the powers of the universe that fulfill individual potential. It is through the transformation of his shadow that he set the pattern for living free from anxiety, guilt, and fear.

Scary Saints and Grasping Gurus

All too often, spiritual leaders fail to transform their lost and broken parts. The result is that they can lead themselves and others sadly astray and do a great deal of harm.

People who are highly developed in some areas may be dwarfs in the most essential ones. Hitler was an extreme example of this. He was cognitively acute, aesthetically sensitive, and socially adept in many ways, but morally depraved. He was conversant with esoteric lore and therefore "spiritual" in a perverted sense, although he interpreted his experience along racial lines and projected his pathological beliefs on the world around him. Because of our capacity to abuse power, the mystics and saints speak of purgation and mortification, processes which really have more to do with pruning the ego than controlling the flesh.

Mystics warn that one can attain the highest mystical states, levitate, or see Christ, and still be a bad egg in the end. This is why the great spiritual teachers place so little value on seeking mystical states for their own sake. The mystics who contribute to the spiritual evolution of humankind have scrutinized themselves for wholeness (or the lack of it), and are slow to claim perfection or enlightenment. They work humbly to make a contribution after confronting multifarious aspects of the self, conscious and unconscious.

The stories of Jesus and other advanced spiritual teachers and wisdom masters like Milarepa or Gautama Buddha have to be re-enacted in each person. The 12th-century Tibetan monk Milarepa, for instance, welcomed his shadow by conversing with his "demons" in a way that was neither accepting nor rejecting but ultimately a channelling of their power for creative ends.[2]

A Big Bear Dream

Back in the early 1980s I had a particularly poignant dream that is one of my most memorable encounters with the shadow. In the dream, my husband and I were attempting to help a group of children board a ship before being assaulted by a ferocious man in a bear costume. He was, I can assure you, more terrifying than any pure animal bear might have been. I titled the poem I wrote about this dream experience "Love Your Enemies."

Love Your Enemies

What if the dreamer surrendered herself
to the scary man in the bear costume?

The children might escape,
leaving the man beating his fists on the ground.

What kind of evil does he portend?
Rape? Murder? Systemic violence?

He is not a person or a country.
His dance of hatred and rage

strips and steals the skins of animals
to disguise a bottomless fear.

Of what is he afraid?
Children's spontaneous laughter,

toothless gums at the breast,
a future that does not know his name?

Perhaps his own emptiness if he halts the offence.
The dreamer stands stock still on the shore

imagining both her certain extermination
and the strange thing love might do

to change the weary, inarticulate
bulk of him, or loosen the knots of his heart

should she take him in her arms.[3]

Fortunately, the dreamer wraps the man in her arms as she would a child, and his costume falls away just before she sees the face. Perhaps it is her own "original face," the one she had before she was born. I can see now that the poem asks the questions that passed through my mind, the questions that kept me from perceiving the man in the bear costume merely as an enemy to be evaded or destroyed. The dreamer has to imagine a different kind of encounter before transformation can ever happen.

    I, you, we all need to embrace and love these incoherent, broken parts of ourselves if we are to be peacemakers in the world and help the next generation move beyond the ancient petty disputes and nationalisms that are rapidly destroying the planet. The world's non-dual mystics, whose lives have become the stuff of myth and legend, have enacted these stories of "enemy-loving" on a world stage. By awakening to our own mystical selves, we too can live more holistic lives and be part of the healing.

1 Bruce Sanguin, "Opening Up as Spiritual Practice," a sermon preached Sept. 6, 2009. http://www.canadianmemorial.org/sermons_2/2009_09_06.html

2 Judith Simmer-Brown, "Inviting the Demon" in *Parabola: Myth, Tradition, and the Search for Meaning: the Shadow,* Vol. XXII, No. 2 (May 1997), 17.

3 Susan McCaslin, *A Plot of Light* (Lantzville, British Columbia: Oolichan Books, 2004), 29.

Chapter Four

The Paradise Ear

In my Father's house there are many dwelling places. If it were not so, would I have told you that I go to prepare a place for you?

~ *JOHN 14:2*

Lucent Prayer

*From our mothers' wombs we came crying
to slopes of green, a vault of sky:*

    Praise and glory to the Most High

*With Spirit we wove our bodies from star
stuff, bodies of frozen light:*

    Praise and glory to the Most Deep

*Open us now to the innermost recesses
where you serenely dwell:*

    Praise and glory to the Most Deep

to the heaven without, within,
the heaven that is both now and to be:

> Praise and glory to the Most Wide

You, beyond all names and naming,
we fall with your falling:

> Praise and glory to the Most Wide

You, transcending our enterprises,
we rise in your rising:

> Praise and glory to
> the Most Spacious One

A few months ago, I attended a gospel choir concert in Vancouver and found myself singing along to the old hymns about "crossing over Jordan" and "going home." Don't get me wrong; I'm not depressed, ready to die, or in need of consolation over the death of a loved one. But somehow the intensity of the longing for a paradise beyond the temporal world as we know it moved me unexpectedly. I began to wonder again if I would see my deceased parents in some future state, where they are now, and whether and in what conditions individual consciousness might survive the death of the body.

Whatever Happened to Heaven?

After years of being non-institutional Christians with solitary prayer and meditation practices, my husband and I became involved with a Christian community that is exploring the best work of non-literalist liberal theologians Marcus Borg, Shelby Spong, John Crossan, and Bruce Chilton, as well as an evolutionary paradigm that takes account of transpersonal states of being and consciousness. I am able to explore an inclusive, multi-faith perspective in which the Christian revelation is only one unique expression of the divine.

However, although the biblical historians and liberal theologians do not necessarily deny the existence of dimensions beyond the material world, somehow reflections on the reality of an afterlife or paradise, whether glimpsed in this life or experienced in another, are not often discussed in their works. There is little focus on what Thomas Merton called "the paradise ear,"[1] an inward attentiveness to the realms of spirit as they manifest in language and in the visible world. I began to wonder if mainstream Protestant Christianity's tendency to ignore its rich heritage of paradisal imagery has not resulted in a diminishment of faith and the loss of one of the profound sources of consolation in religious life – the paradigm of paradise.

The word consolation can be problematic. Doesn't it suggest that intuition about heaven is a pie-in-the-sky illusion, an escapist refusal to accept death, and a denial of the reality of this world? The old dualism of heaven versus earth has not served us well and has led to many abuses. Perhaps we need to just get used to the idea that "when you're dead, you're dead," or at best recycled into the cosmic soup. After all, isn't the desire to see individual consciousness continue at the egoic level a fairly self-centred wish? And what if we do enter oblivion or return to the vast oneness when our brain cells die? Why not just take comfort in doing our part to leave a positive legacy, live fully in the present moment, and accept death when it comes?

In fact, from a historical perspective there are many good reasons for mistrusting the old theologies of transcendence and the accompanying promises of heaven. One is the legitimate concern that emphasis on otherworldliness distracts us from building a better world for ourselves and our descendants in the here and now. Belief in an afterlife has been used to justify the status quo and legitimize corrupt hegemonic systems. I shall never forget my dismay at hearing James Watts, the Secretary of the Interior under Ronald Reagan, argue that we don't need to worry about pollution or saving trees since this world will be burned up anyway in the fires of Armageddon and Christ will deliver the Christians to a heavenly safety zone. Otherworldly theology has sought to justify the unjustifiable by deferring to the beyond. Perhaps the liberal theologians avoid the discourse of transcendence because it is associated with the old paradigm that tolerates inaction and political malfeasance and places God outside rather than within the world.

Many Dimensions

In contrast to the primarily linear and historical approach of many liberal theologians, the testimony of the major religions and the traditions of the mystics suggest a multidimensional universe in which this world and other interior worlds are mysteriously intertwined. In most world religions, the geography of other worlds is a significant part of their cosmology, and most assume an intimate interconnection between this world and another, with the larger more cohesive spiritual order informing and permeating the material one. To dismiss experiences of and intuitions about an afterlife or more inclusive realms of consciousness is to ignore a central stream in world religious experience. Postmodern materialists, skeptics about life-beyond-death, are in the minority in terms of the history of religion through the ages.

To have glimpses of heaven in the beauty of a wildflower or a grain of sand does not necessarily preclude social action; such glimpses of heaven within earth can create the desire to act justly if we believe that what is begun in time carries on. A cosmology that assumes the interconnectedness of all realms heightens the sense of the importance of acting ethically in the present. To live in the present moment is to be present to the eternal worlds, since this world is part of and permeated by the eternal order. The timeless dwells within this world and this world within the timeless. Therefore, we try to act according to the highest we know because all worlds are part of a larger whole and what we do has resonance in many dimensions. Eternity and time are two perspectives on a single reality.

Life in Flatland

Why, then, have people so easily relinquished the transcendent aspect of religion? One reason is that we have become infected with a limited empiricism that makes an ideology of the notion that there is no anterior order beyond the realm of the fives senses. Many scientists are not yet open to the idea of more inclusive, integral, or timeless dimensions. I would suggest that awe at the big bang as an event in time that gave birth to the material universe is not a substitute for a spirituality that encompasses transcendence or a causal realm of creative Spirit. Brian Swimme and other contemporary cosmologists seek to reconcile scientific inquiry and more mystical perception. They propose an awe-inspiring picture of the material universe as a bio-spiritual reality.

Secondly, because it can be difficult to distinguish between madness and visionary states, there is a natural fear of reports of life-beyond-death and the spiritual realms. But a blurring between psycho-mental imbalance and visionary consciousness does not mean they are identical. The mystical traditions offer ways to identify authentic visionary awareness, although there has been a tendency to pathologize the mystics. The raptures and locutions of Teresa of Avila, the 16th-century Spanish mystic, for instance, have been treated as symptoms of hysteria by the Freudians. However, such approaches fail to examine authentic mystical experience as the root and ground of organized religion.

Since mainstream religion rarely engages questions about the life-beyond-death and mystical perceptions, New Age ideology has tended to appropriate this area. People are drawn to channeling or conversing with the dead (watered down forms of ancient, esoteric teaching) because intuitions about the continuity of consciousness after death are not often discussed in mainline churches.

Longing for a Paradise Both Here and Beyond

Despite liberal theology's silence regarding cosmographies of heaven, Jesus kept telling his disciples about the

Kingdom of Heaven. He saw this kingdom through visionary awareness and spent much of his time trying to convey it to his followers through metaphor.

In a sense, we are the kingdom of heaven here and now: we are Christ in the making, male and female alike. Another way of expressing this is, "Christ is being formed in us." God is in us and in nature; yet God is beyond our knowing. Blake saw heaven in a grain of sand; yet heaven is also beyond our senses and temporal perceptions. What is important is that we remain open to the possibility of paradise both here and beyond and say yes to such glimpses and do not shut them down prematurely. For without attending to our interior vision of a just and peaceful world, we have no models on which to make the world a better place. Imagination is primary, not something merely for idealists and dreamers. We must first imagine a place where love rules in order to become active in making such a state of non-violence palpable. In a very real sense, what we imagine we become. For me as a poet (and I believe all of us are inherently creative beings or artists in some way), paradise is the experience of being on the cutting edge of divine creativity where the operative phrase is always "behold, I make all things new."

Breakfast with Dad

Without seeking life-beyond-death experiences, I have found that encounters with those who have passed over have occurred at crucial times in my life, particularly in association with the deaths of my parents. My father died at the age of sixty-six after a long struggle with Lou Gehrig's disease, or ALS. He suffered a devastating deterioration of the nerves that control the muscles, leaving him a human shipwreck unable to lift his head and barely able to speak. Just before he died, Dad told me that he had had a dream where he found himself hurtling across space to the other side of the universe – fearless, exhilarated, and curious about what came next.

Six years after his death, Dad appeared to me in the state between dreaming and waking. He was serving me breakfast at a big oak table like the one we had at home when I was a kid. He had prepared his favourite thing – what he called the Saturday Morning Super-Dooper Wing-Ding Breakfast. He had spread out strips of greasy bacon, hunks of sausage, fried eggs, mounds of buttered toast, hash browns, grapefruit, prunes, milk, juice, marmalade, jams, and a big jar of peanut butter.

One surprising feature of this dream-vision was that Dad seemed to have aged backward. He appeared at the head of his ample breakfast table as if breaking the fast of our not seeing one another. The other outstanding detail was that he sat shirtless at the table. I realized later that this was to show me that he had completely regained the musculature that had been ravaged by the wasting disease. I will never forget his infectious smile, as if he had organized this banquet as a huge surprise.

I wrote about my visionary experience of first seeing him again at breakfast in an unpublished poem:

Postscript: Visionary Father

Six years and nothing,
(my vagrant ineffective cries)
not a day without thought of you.

This morning you break (fast) with me
suddenly, sunny side up.
The shine of you, the glare.
How is it you dare to be younger
than I, your middle-aged self?
What do they grow in neverland
that makes you glow?

*We have reversed ourselves —
you drew me here
then left for there.
I am here in your there
communing with you now.*

*How your growing backwards
surpasses me, your skin's peach
and dew more real than fingered stone.*

*But if I reach to touch or speak
the power breaks and you go sliding back
like the ghost you are not
into the fullness you have become.*[2]

Belly-Laughing with My Mom

In addition, my mother, who had struggled with schizophrenia much of her life, became more and more at peace with herself in her last years at a nursing home. Though deeply sunk in dementia, she seemed to be contained within a sort of aura of well-being that overcame her long-term anxiety. Her troubles could not destroy her enormous laughter and her ability to make others laugh – these remained with her till almost the end. When I got the call that she was dying I rushed to her bedside. I had the distinct sense she was somehow seeking my permission to go, so I told her that if it was her time to leave us she should, but that nothing could ever separate those who truly love each other. Though she didn't seem to comprehend at the time, that night she quietly ceased breathing. A few weeks later my husband, who is quite psychic, saw her laughing and talking in a room of people, sitting in a chair and swinging her legs like a girl. He felt she had been living partly in the mundane world of the nursing home and partly in a parallel world for about a year before she was ready to go on. But the time had come and she was able to slip easily into the folds of the next world.

Not Belief, but Experience

The purpose of opening to such awareness is not to build new beliefs and doctrines about heaven or the afterlife but to honour our epiphanies, those direct experiences that suggest the material world is not the whole of reality. When we read the story of the Ascension of Jesus to the status of the Christ we begin to "ascend with Christ," hopeful that the death of the physical body is not the end of the story. In the Lord's Prayer, Jesus' emphasis is also clear: "Thy kingdom come; thy will be done, *on earth, as it is in heaven.*" These words imply that our vision of heaven combined with our love for the earth is the foundation for the building of the kingdom of heaven on earth. Jesus affirms the reality of heaven as a dynamic state of higher consciousness but also emphasizes that it is up to us to will it into being here and now – to "will the transformation." The kingdom both *is* and *is to come.* This world, perceived rightly, is heaven, but not the whole of heaven.

So it is essential to keep alive our paradisal visions of this world and the next. We can do this by revisiting some of our traditional images of heaven, reclaiming them for our time, discussing those that are destructive or exclusionary, and developing new myths of ecstasy, glory, and bliss. Recovering the paradisal imagery and corresponding experiential knowledge in our own tradition could be a portal for connection to other faith traditions. For instance, how is the Buddhist notion of nirvana like and unlike the Christian hope for heaven? What do the visionaries Emanuel Swedenborg and Jacob Boehme have to say to us now about an afterlife?

Thousands of ordinary people all over the world testify to communing directly with deceased loved ones. Nurses provide anecdotal reports of near-death experiences. Those who have been declared clinically dead report being transformed by their experience of another life. Developments in science, medicine, and physics have led some neurologists and neurosurgeons to reconsider their materialist assumptions. Although the distinction between the mind and the brain cannot be proved by discursive reason, almost every major religion has alluded to a form of consciousness that transcends death.

Death or Transformation?

While evolutionary Christianity needs to distance itself from the literalism of fundamentalism, a willingness to re-examine the deep longing for a paradise beyond this world in the Christian tradition may speak to the need to ask such questions as, "Where am I going? Is the mind more than the brain? Is there a world or worlds beyond the one I can taste, see, and measure?" Why should fundamentalism offer simplistic answers that encourage self-righteousness and us-them thinking, while so-called progressive Christians merely give these questions a polite nod? The Christian mystical heritage is filled with treasures that might open us to timeless mystery and offer not only comfort but fountains of wisdom. Perhaps the image of crossing over Jordan into the arms of light can have renewed meaning for us in our common movement toward death, or, just possibly, transformation.

---

1 Thomas Merton, "Louis Zukofsky—the Paradise Ear," in *The Literary Essays of Thomas Merton*. (Ed. Patrick Hart; New York: New Directions, 1981). Merton uses the phrase "the paradise ear" to talk about the poetics of American poet Louis Zukofsky.

2 Susan McCaslin. An unpublished poem from the cycle "Main Street Elegies."

Chapter Five

Countering War with Wonder

To see a World in a Grain of Sand
And a Heaven in a Wild flower:
Hold Infinity in the palm of your hand
And Eternity in an hour.[1]

~ *WILLIAM BLAKE*

Compassionate One,

*Parse us your beauty in the particulars:
striped red tulips by a gate,*

*Perseid meteor showers in an August sky,
the steady progress of a banana slug across
   the driveway.*

*Notice in us. Be our hearing, touching,
tasting, smelling, seeing. Burn*

*as we co-create with You in one
continuous act of creation*

*so that we, piecemeal, may become Your peace,
building new Jerusalems in the ruins.*

~ ~ ~ Susan McCaslin ~ ~ ~

The imaginative power of humans and their innate desire to make things of use and beauty have coexisted alongside impulses toward defensiveness, aggression, and greed throughout human history. Sometimes people have harnessed their creative propensities to the engines of war, producing patriotic paintings depicting the glory of battle, but more often artists transform human conflict in ways that are more life-affirming. When a person is absorbed deeply in a creative act like furniture-making, music-making, or poetry-making, she may experience joy, exhilaration, or sorrow, but the more aggressive, reptilian brain responses are dimmed. I think certain forms of art have the power to prompt us toward peace because they are ultimately acts of creation made through the power of love, in which every molecule of the artist's mind has turned toward receptivity and attention. For the creator of such works, the entire being is absorbed in the process of bringing something to birth in beauty and amazement. English poet and painter William Blake is one of those rare visionary artists whose imaginative vision counters war with wonder.

An artist who shapes alternative realities that enrich life cannot, in the moment of creation at least, be a warrior primed to kill. And those who respond to the creative arts can be gently pivoted toward peace through their active participation in a vision of the world that refuses to see things in terms of self and other, black and white, good guys and bad. Such art steps back and takes a broader view in which diverse things are richly interconnected. In its most complex and meaningful forms, sacred art evokes empathy and compassion. Yet the artist can also be called to what Blake called the "mental fight," a form of spiritual warfare where the opponent is everything within and without that hinders the expansiveness of creative imagination in both the individual and society.

Waging Imaginative Warfare

Blake, writing at the end of the Enlightenment in the early 19th century, urged that we should cultivate Imaginative contentions, not physical ones. (He usually capitalized the word Imagination to distinguish it from mere fancy.) Like the poet Coleridge, who wrote that Imagination is "the repetition in the finite mind of the eternal act of creation in the Infinite I AM,"[2] Blake saw the imagination as our primary means of union with ultimate reality. He argued that if every man and every woman were engaged in acts of creative Imagination war would eventually cease and we would have commenced the task of building the New Jerusalem, a spiritual community based on mutual forgiveness. John Lennon, another radical idealist like Blake, urged, "Make love, not war," and "Give peace a chance." Blake might have added, "Make art, not weapons of mass destruction."

The English poet followed with intense interest the revolutions that were occurring in America and France when he was a young man, and applauded these social upheavals as necessary to bring about social justice. He wore the red cap of supporters of the French Revolution for a time and was considered a radical or a sympathizer with radicals. But like John Lennon and others who stepped back from the tumult of their era to observe the spiral of violence spinning out from the revolution, Blake soon became disillusioned when he witnessed the replacing of one reign of terror with another. He therefore later denounced violent revolution and opted for an imaginative transformation of society that must begin within each individual.

If we could only perceive the world "not with but through the eye," he mused,[3] a tree would no longer appear as a number of board feet of lumber, but a being of sentience and light: "The fool sees not the same tree that a wise man sees."[4] The sun would not resemble a coin or guinea in the sky, but "a host of heavenly angels singing Holy, Holy, Holy."[5] If "everything that lives is holy,"[6] and if we experience this holiness from our innermost core, then we will not be inclined to destroy the natural world that is our matrix. The desire to manipulate the world as if it were other would fade, and the need to dominate our fellow creatures might become unthinkable.

Blake's Imagination is much more than an organ of aesthetic appreciation. The Imagination is the act of seeing through what the East has called third-eye vision, and what Blake called four-fold vision. It is an act of being in which mind, body, emotions, and creative imagination are integrated by the creative faculty, the same divine mind that continually gives birth to the cosmos and that is repeated in us. Blake's mythology is a cosmology in which the individual moves into balance to become not just an autonomous bit of mechanism in a clockwork universe but a repetition of the movements of the cosmos, a microcosm participating in a glorious dance. Every flower, tree, person, and grain of sand is a centre capable of expanding to infinity where one can see "a world in a grain of sand."

Blake's Jesus

The figure of Jesus in Blake's system is the Imagination awake in each of us – the "Divine Humanity." Crabb Robinson, one of Blake's contemporaries, reported in his journal that when asked if Jesus was the divine Son of God, Blake retorted, "He is the only God – but so am I and so are you."[7] Though his words probably sounded like blasphemy to Crabb, what Blake meant is that each of us is a potential embodiment of what can be called the Christ-consciousness. Artists like Blake, who seem crazy to some, can be prophets calling us to a more authentic mode of being.

Despite his lack of recognition in his lifetime, Blake was reported to have died in a glorious burst of song. Though poor and unrecognized, he was exuberant, as if he had gazed deeply into the heart of things. For him, the callings of poet and prophet (visionary and social critic) are one and the same, for he exposes in his art the devastating effects of the Industrial Revolution and the widening gap between rich and poor. Here the exploited chimney sweeper of *Songs of Experience* speaks in corrosive irony:

> And because I am happy, & dance and sing,
> They think they have done me no injury:
> And are gone to praise God & his Priest & King
> Who make up a heaven of our misery.[8]

Blake's Postmodern Cosmology

Blake's work is still studied in colleges and universities around the world over 250 years since his birth, but society at large has not caught up with him. The social ills he blazoned are now magnified on a global scale. The Enlightenment scientism he interrogated in his attack on Newton, Lock, and Bacon has invented the atomic bomb, so-called smart bombs, and chemical warfare. It has furthered the them/us, subject/object thinking that sets us (and God or the divine) outside the natural world and under the illusion that we can control it for our use. Greed, exploitation, warfare, the demonizing of the other, and false religion in the form of militant fundamentalisms are now endangering not just England but the globe's fragile ecosystems. The smog over industrial London has exploded into an envelope of greenhouse gas emissions that now threaten the balance of life on the planet.

Blake depicts the progress of this kind of destructiveness in his epic poem "Jerusalem." Yet his genius is that he transforms the apocalyptic narratives of the Bible into psychodramas of interior transformation. He writes that when anyone embraces truth and casts off error, a "last judgment" occurs within the person on the spot.[9] Judgment for Blake is not a punishment by an angry God but a sloughing off of error or mistakes – a form of liberation.

There is a release from states that no longer serve. No one who chooses to be free is forever locked in a hell of his or her own making in Blake's universe.

Blake leaves us with hope. Jesus the Imagination restores fallen Reason (Blake's Urizen) to his proper place in human consciousness. The male and female aspects of each person embrace. And this reunion occurs through acts of empathy, compassion, and mutual forgiveness.

Blake's whole cosmic narrative is a re-visioning of the Fall and redemption. He suggests that a broken-off or "fallen" form of reason has usurped its place in the collective psyche and wreaked havoc, but through the awakening of creative Imagination in each we can restore our right relation to the earth and to the larger community, symbolized as Jerusalem. He believes that transformation of a few will eventually lead to a transformation of the public realm. But we are not to wait for a divine *fiat* or "let it be" from God, for we contain within us the power to change the world. Such a recognition of the infinite in the creation is the artist's gift, and those who participate in the arts become co-creators of new, life-altering ways of perceiving and living.

The Transformative Arts

If poetry, painting, and music are "the three Powers in Man of conversing with Paradise,"[10] as Blake states, why do the arts fail to move society irrevocably towards justice and peace? For without justice, external peace can become a false ideal, a deceiving harmony or adjustment to corruption that actually covers up injustice. Mere aesthetic appreciation, it seems, can happily coexist with the most abhorrent forms of inhumanity. For instance, German audiences flocked to concerts and theatrical performances, refining their aesthetic sensibilities, where a few paces away Jews were dying in concentration camps. The modernist poet Ezra Pound could pen *The Cantos* and yet work for Mussolini's radio station, believing he was opposing the usurious banking system. The ability to appreciate and create art is no anodyne for complicity with systemic evil, whether one is involved with corruption directly or indirectly. A love for the arts does not necessarily guarantee prescience or an advanced ethos.

In Blake's mythology, art corrupted corrupts society and no longer performs its prophetic function, its role as witness. Sometimes all an artist has to do his let his or her art mirror the horrors of an injustice, so people can choose how they will respond. For Blake, visionary and prophetic art is a refining fire. Such artists labour like blacksmiths at their forges to make art that (implicitly or explicitly) indicts corruption and offers an alternative vision. "Would to God that all the Lord's people were Prophets,"[11] cries Blake. And he adds in "Jerusalem," let everyone "as much as in him lies engage himself openly and publicly before all the World in some Mental pursuit for the building up of Jerusalem."[12]

Prophetic, visionary poetry like Blake's is an art of social engagement that does not allow us to compartmentalize life. It cracks us open, softens our hearts, and transforms. As the voice of a sculpture by Rodin whispers to the poet Rilke, "You must change your life."[13]

Certainly we can resist the way visionary art works on us, but prophetic art provides a portal to new ways of being. Such art declares, "Enter at your peril, or the risk of your egocentric self." If art took on again its prophetic function, those who are reluctant to come to the arts because they find them inaccessible or see them merely as frills or decoration might have to reconsider.

Art of the Blakean sort surpasses mere entertainment but is nevertheless compelling, often disturbing. The artist's form of social criticism is in the end more effective than any form of political invective because it invokes the whole self in both the one who creates and the one who reads, sees, or hears. Such art creates a dynamic between the thing or issue depicted and the audience that is a kind of "third space" where the "whole being" is called into presence.

Poetry, though a marginalized form today, except perhaps in rap lyrics or popular song, has the advantage of appealing to many levels of our being at once: the world of imagery, the world of musicality (sound, rhythm), and the world of thought and meaning. In a good poem all three are up and running. Discursive prose moves mainly at the level of idea; but poetry, music, and painting interweave all three levels to activate the body, mind, emotions, and Spirit simultaneously. Sometimes a magical synesthesia, or blending of the senses, can come into play. Because of the power of the arts to speak to our deepest interiority, Blake speaks of art as having the power to awake: "Awake! Awake O sleeper in the land of shadows, wake! Expand!"[14]

Poetry and Peacemaking

How, then, does poetry restore us to peace? Is there a poetry of peace? I would suggest that visionary poetry is a mode of contemplation in which one moves fluidly from interiority and silence to expression. In a painting or poem the silences are as important (more important perhaps) as the images or words. Art calls us to contemplation and contemplation calls us back to action or creative response. Contemplation stirs the soul to action and action to contemplation. One need not choose one or the other, but follow as Spirit leads. St. Teresa of Avila and John of the Cross, both mystics of deep interior silences, knew well the limits of language when it came to talking about God or the divine, but also continued to write glorious poetry. At the end of his life, St. Francis wrote "The Canticle of the Creatures," a hymn to the sun, moon, stars, and wild animals. What poetry can do, then, is to lead us up to the very brink of the invisible, the ineffable, the nameless, and allow us to sink briefly into the divine unity. Then it draws us back from that silence with burning hearts and lips and gives us back to the world.

1. William Blake, from "Auguries of Innocence" in *Blake's Poetry and Designs* (Mary Lynn Johnson and John E. Grant, ed.; New York: Norton, 1979), 209.

2. Samuel Taylor Coleridge, from *Biographia Literaria,* Chapter XIII in English Romantic Writers. (David Perkins, ed.; New York: Harcourt, 1967), 452.

3. Blake, from "The Everlasting Gospel" in *Blake's Poetry and Designs,* 368.

4. Blake, from "The Marriage of Heaven and Hell" in *Blake's Poetry and Designs,* 89.

5. Blake, from "A Vision of the Last Judgment" in *Blake's Poetry and Designs,* 416.

6. Blake, from "The Marriage" in *Blake's Poetry and Designs,* 102.

7. Blake, from Henry Crabb Robinson's *Reminiscences* (1852), 497.

8. Ibid, 46.

9. Blake, from "A Vision of the Last Judgment" in *Blake's Poetry and Designs,* 413.

10. Ibid, 412.

11. Blake, "Milton," Plate 1, 239.

12. Blake, "Jerusalem" in *Blake's Poetry and Designs,* 346–347.

13. Rainer Maria Rilke, "Archaic Torso of Apollo," *The Selected Poetry of Rainer Maria Rilke* (Stephen Mitchell, ed.; New York: Random House, 1989), 61.

14. Blake, from "Jerusalem," Chap. 1, 313.

Chapter Six

Rapturous Ravishments

Let him kiss me with the kisses of his mouth!
For your love is more delightful than wine,
Your anointing oils are fragrant,
your name is perfume poured out.

~ SONG OF SONGS, 1:2–3

Responsive Song

Come home, my people.
We come home from the daily warfare.

Come home, beloved.
We come home from the clenched jaw.

Come home, my lovers.
We come home from the inauthentic dream.

Come home, dear friends.
*We come home from the deserts of
  too much busyness.*

Come home, brothers and sisters.
*We are home in your garden of
   pomegranates.*

Come home, my fair ones.
We are home in the wine of your laughter.

Come home, lost companions.
We are home in your banqueting hall.

Come home, my deeply beloved ones.
We are home in the birthright of loving.

From the author of the Song of Solomon or Song of Songs to the Islamic Sufi mystics Rabi'a and Rumi, and the Hindu mystic Mirabai, poets have compared union with God (the source of "all that is") to the union of a lover and a beloved partner. This kind of metaphor is risky business, as it seems to reduce the spiritual to the sensual or invite us to confuse them. Yet there is no more apt and pure symbolism for mystical union, since the love that unites two people sexually can be a manifestation of the same love that holds the cosmos together. It is no wonder that mystics across cultures have used erotic symbolism and the metaphors of betrothal, marriage, and sexual consummation to describe the states of mystical union.

The poets Rumi and Kabir often symbolize God as the Beloved. Rumi writes, "My being is but a goblet in the Beloved's hand – look at my eyes, if you do not believe it."[1] In other places he presents God as the Lover or the burning love that dwells within the core of being and into which the ego disappears or is "annihilated." In his poetry, as in the Song of Songs, the relationship between the human and the divine is fluid and interchangeable.

Sometimes in the physical act of love it is difficult to discern who is who. In his poem "You Have the Lovers" Leonard Cohen writes, "When he puts his mouth against her shoulder / she is uncertain whether her shoulder / has given or received the kiss."[2] In spiritual union too, one can't say who gives and who receives, for the boundaries of the divine and the self have melted away.

But lest we think only contemporary, edgy poets tease us in this way, check out the over the top sensuality of the Song of Songs:

> My beloved thrust his hand into the opening,
> and my inmost being yearned for him.
> I arose to open to my beloved,
> and my hands dripped with myrrh,
> my fingers with liquid myrrh,
> upon the handles of the bolt.
>
> ~ SONG OF SONGS, 5:4–5

The nation Israel in the Hebrew Bible is often compared to a beloved bride, and the imagery migrated into Christianity as the Bride of Christ. In his parables, Jesus depicts the kingdom of heaven on earth as a festive marriage banquet, a celebration of a union between loving partners, and his first miracle takes place at a wedding with plenty of wine.

What all this does is sanctify sex and intimacy and show that when they happen between two people who love, respect, and trust each other, human union participates in the divine consummation of all things with their creative source. There is a momentary disappearance of ego, an ecstatic drawing together. Physical union becomes a mirror image for spiritual union. When humans enter into a loving relationship, then, they are re-enacting what is happening constantly between the original unity and the fragmented parts of creation. There are no gender wars here, for in love the weapons of destruction are laid down. The crux is whether or not one can be vulnerable enough to step into love's fire.

Ravishment Versus Rapine

When one experiences the unspeakable rush of pure being as transcendence, it feels like being lifted to a higher level. Before the One, the only thing to do is surrender the old self and be swept up or ravished. This is not rape. Rape is an act of violation of the body and soul, while ravishment is a willing entrance into the bliss of ecstatic fusion. In the Song of Songs, where the bride is as active in pursuit of her beloved as the beloved is of her, eroticism implies mutuality and consent.

Sacred Love

In contemporary culture, where such a thing as bridal mysticism or talk of sacred sexuality is rare, one has to ask, into what kind of sexuality are our youth inducted? I recall when the time came to speak to my daughter about the "facts of life" I was concerned about informing her of the dangers of unwanted pregnancy, sexually transmitted diseases, and inappropriate touching by adults. And it is certainly proper to teach our children to protect themselves against sexual risks or abuse. However, how often do we convey, either verbally or through our actions, that the intimate exchange of love between two consenting adults can be both a transcendent and an into-the-body experience, an act of beauty that connects us with our deepest core and the core of the universe? How often do we discuss the importance of nurturing a relationship through its highs and lows, or speak about true love as entering into a process in which two selves empty themselves into a whole greater than any idea they might have had of themselves to begin with?

As a species, we can treat sex as a reproductive function, a means of procreation, a source of pleasure and loving exchange, and as something that may include and transcend all of these. Perhaps the "small death" of surrender in love is a prelude to the larger surrender of ourselves to the mysterious ways of the cosmos, the realization of how deeply and intimately the universe loves us.

The Sexiest Book in the Bible

When I first encountered the luscious language of the Song of Songs at around age 17, I was drawn in not only by its frank eroticism, but also by the sense of blissful abandonment to the power of love. I knew in my bones that this was poetry at its most sensuous: "Sustain me with raisins, refresh me with apples: for I am faint with love. / O that his left hand were under my head, and that his right hand embraced me!" (2:5–6).

Years later, I began to wonder how such wild imagery could have made it into the Bible in the first place. Scholars still have not decided whether the Song is an erotic love poem (possibly based in pagan, Middle Eastern rituals celebrating the nuptials of a god and goddess), a simple celebration of human sexuality, or an allegory or metaphor for spiritual union.

It turns out the Song of Songs was only included in the Bible after it was allegorized as the union of God with Israel. Yet if the Song is a holy text, it is one that upholds the value of sexuality and the body. Alicia Ostricker, poet and feminist theologian, calls the Song a countertext because it "resists dominant structures of authority, divine and legal," as generally represented in the Bible.[3] The woman's experience is at the centre of the poem and she is presented as Solomon's equal. Her desire parallels his, as do her speeches of praise for his beauty and her ability to express pleasure in her own sensuality. And though these two lovers are relatively balanced in terms of power, power is not the issue, for the whole desire is to relinquish it into the keeping of the other.

In their world of sensuous indwelling, the lovers are interwoven with the natural world, being compared to ewes, horses, and gazelles. The locale of their drama is a lush, Edenic garden overflowing with pomegranates, apricots, and apples that practically cascade from the weighted trees. We are enveloped in a pastoral world of abundance where the line "love is strong as death" (8:6) is affirmed in the imagery. The book functions as a countertext to the story of Adam and Eve in Genesis because here the woman is active in her relation to her counterpart and their sensuality is not presented as problematic or fallen. The sensual and secular, the spiritual and sacred, are united.

The Song of Songs suggests that Spirit is more like a lover than a lawgiver or judge, and that being in interconnection with the divine is more like falling in love than living up to an external standard of rightness. It asks:

What if the intelligence of the universe is constantly wooing us and enticing us into meaning in order to fill us with radiant glory and fulfill every bit of our potential? Finally, it offers a model of what the ancients called a *conjunctio oppositorum,* or union of opposites, that demonstrates love without violence. Love is a gentle call, a loving reciprocity that wishes to infuse us with delight and an enhancement of being. Like the mysterious Beloved, love advances and retreats, sometimes disappearing; yet it will suddenly return in newness. In this dance, humans are both lover and beloved, as is the equally mysterious Godhead. No matter what our sexual or gender orientation, the images point to the eros of relationship as a love-longing that draws the fragmented parts of things together.

Teresa's Transverberation

The 16th-century Spanish mystic Teresa of Avila goes further than any of the medieval saints who reworked the imagery of the Song of Songs when she describes in intimate detail her own interior erotic experiences of the divine – the *toques de union* or touches of union of the heavenly bridegroom. Teresa was ordered by her superiors to write her entire story, a command which resulted in her autobiography *La Vida.* The section in which she describes her erotic experience has been called the Transverberation, an embarrassment to some and fodder for the Freudian mill for others. Bernini's well-known statue *The Ecstasy of St. Teresa* depicts the saint with her head tipped back and her mouth agape in an expression of utter orgasmic release. Though religious interpretations insist the ecstasy is purely spiritual, the famous passage where Teresa describes a "short but very beautiful" angel of the realm of the Seraphim is not for the Puritanical or faint of heart:

> In his [the angel's] hands I saw a great golden spear, and at the iron tip there appeared to be a point of fire. This he plunged into my heart several times so that it penetrated to my entrails. When he pulled it out, I felt that he took them with it, and left me utterly consumed by the great love of God. The pain was so severe that it made me utter several moans. The sweetness caused by this intense pain is so extreme that one cannot possibly wish it to cease, nor is one's soul then content with anything but God. This is not a physical, but a spiritual pain, though the body has some share in it – even a considerable share. So gentle is this wooing which takes place between God and the soul that if anyone thinks I am lying, I pray God, in His goodness, to grant him some experience of it.[4]

We have to smile at the nun's subtle warning to her confessors that they can't speak with authority of such rapturous raptures without having known them. And although the body shares in the experience, the experience itself cannot be reduced to merely physical and psychic sensation.

Years ago, I found myself in dialogue with Teresa while writing a sequence called *The Teresa Poems,* where Teresa takes up her quarrel with the Freudians who would reduce her experience to sublimated sexuality. As the poems emerged, I found myself amused at her feisty tone.

I Have a Few Words to Say to the Freudians

about the event in my story
referred to as the "Transverberation,"

the "flaming heart" Crashaw in his poem
got so worked up over 200 years afterward.

I mean, that angelic piercing,
those darts of core-driven light,

all that fusion of pleasure and pain.
You might as well know

there are some ecstasies
having little to do with sex

though we steal whatever analogies we can,
and sex is sometimes a whisper

of what I'm talking about.
Erotics within erotics,

bodies in bodies, sheaths in sheaths,
touches of union everywhere so delicate

they imprint the soul with longing.
Yes, there are sublimations, Freud,

having nothing to do with repression,
as the open mouth and the half-closed eyes

of the Bernini in Rome only half suggest.
But you have to try them to know them.[5]

Like all the mystics, Teresa invites us into direct experience of the unspeakable.

Night of Ecstasy

When I was in my early twenties I met the Christian mystic Olga Park, who in her later years began to share with a few people some of the profound mystical experiences she had been having all her life. After I had studied contemplative prayer and meditation with Olga for at least two years, she shared an earlier experience of what she called her "night of ecstasy." I was quite surprised, but had read some of the mystics like Teresa who had had similar experiences of such divine visitations, so had some context. She talked briefly of how the delicacy and intensity of the experience was so exquisite and so much beyond ordinary sexuality as to be completely indescribable. However, it began and was grounded in the body.

It seems to me a mystic can be a catalyst to mystical states in others, for soon after Olga related her story, I experienced something similar. Of course, skeptics would say I only had the experience due to the power of suggestion, but one has to ask what kind of dynamic is at play (beyond the obvious psychological one) when the presence of a teacher or guru acts as a catalyst for growth in a student. The experience began as a gentle tingling at the base of the spine and moved from toe to crown all night long in a timeless state. Later, I discovered parallels between my experience and what the Eastern traditions call *kundalini*, the opening of the *chakras* or sacred energy centres of the body. Why this happened to me I have no idea, except that I had a regular meditation practice in place at the time and was in weekly association with Olga. Perhaps not coincidentally, the event occurred just prior to my meeting the man who was to become my life partner. Yet the invisible lover who whispered *Désirée* into my inner ear remains a mystery.

Poetry can suggest this heightened mode of being more evocatively than prose, and I have written several poems about it. However, because I didn't explain the context at the time, few people realized it was grounded in direct mystical experience.

Psyche

*Obscure and rare that state to which I fell
or rose, no, floated awake into your invisible arms.*

*You whispered, Désirée, and touched me with
  a thousand
exquisite fingers – a rush like hummingbird wings*

*filtering through every parcel from crown
  to toe to crown,
crescendoing, falling, continuing night's
  extravagant enterprise*

*when we flowed and spiraled in the chakras of
  the spine,
blossomed in the thousand-petalled lotus of
  the brain.*

*You were not in and out and away like
any ordinary lover,
but lingered all night, sequestering, calling
me Beloved.*[6]

Placing the night in the context of mystical marriage has helped me embrace it as more than sublimation – a mystery of higher consciousness common to humanity, a gift of the Spirit.

If we cannot dismiss the experiences of people like Teresa, Olga, and maybe even an ordinary writer in British Columbia, who knows what centres of subtle consciousness lie hidden within all of us? The procreative *eros* transmutes into subtle forms of eroticism and creativity on an ascending scale something like a musical one. Though my own experience has never been repeated (once in a lifetime is more than anyone can expect!), it is as alive for me as if it happened yesterday. It serves as a reminder that we are all created for love, in love, by love, and that love wants to permeate us tip to toe. As the Song of Songs puts it, "I am my beloved's and his desire is for me" (7:10).

1   Jalal al-din Rumi, *Mystical Poems of Rumi* (Trans. A.J. Arberry; Chicago: Univ. of Chicago Press, 1968), 50.

2   Leonard Cohen, *Stranger Music: Selected Poems and Song* (Toronto: McClelland & Stewart, 1993), 23–24.

3   Alicia Ostriker, *For the Love of God: the Bible as an Open Book* (New Brunswick: Rutgers University Press, 2007), 18–19.

4   Teresa of Avila, *The Life of Saint Teresa of Avila by Herself* (Trans. J.M. Cohen; NY: Penguin, 1957), 210.

5   Susan McCaslin, *The Altering Eye* (Ottawa, Ontario: Borealis Press, 2000), 23–24. Note: Richard Crashaw, the 17th-century metaphysical poet, wrote a lengthy poem about St. Teresa of Avila called *The Flaming Heart*.

6   Susan McCaslin, "Psyche" in *Lifting the Stone* (Toronto: Seraphim Editions, 2007), 28. I have also written of this experience in the poems "A Night of Ecstasy" and "A Cylinder of Light" from *A Plot of Light* (Lantzville, British Columbia: Oolichan Books) 2004.

Chapter Seven

The Palace of Presence

You are the light of the world. A city built on a hill cannot be hid. No one after lighting a lamp puts it under the bushel basket, but on the lampstand, and it gives light to all in the house. In the same way, let your light shine before others, so that they may see your good works and give glory to your Father in heaven.

~ MATTHEW 5:14–16

Whoever has an ear for this should listen carefully!
Light shines out from the centre of a being of light
and illuminates the whole cosmos.
Whoever fails to become light is a source of darkness.

~ THE GOSPEL OF THOMAS, LOGION 24

Holy One,

*We open now to the mystery
of how your voice sometimes speaks in our
hearts, and how at others
we find you in welling silence.*

*Lift us from the prison of fear
to the palace of presence,
gently release us
from whatever stops us from shining our light.*

*Flare out in us expansively,
so we may become living lamps
set high on lampstands,
vital candles illuminating the entire room.*

*Use our times of uncertainty and doubt
as occasions for growth
so we can mediate your Presence,
triumphing over the wrecks of all our lost Edens.*

*Help us to be like Jesus,
generously pouring out the wine of life,
or like a magnolia blossom
dreaming its own white magnificence.*

*Let us be, Holy One,
like a lotus flower
whose beauty glows the more exquisitely
against the darkness of the depths that
    brought it forth.*

While travelling in Cappadocia in Turkey, a place where early Christians huddled in caves for fear of persecution by the Romans, I had a pretty amazing dream about interfaith dialogue. In the dream, I'm attending an inter-spiritual conference taking place in a large white house somewhere in the Middle East. Representatives from various spiritual traditions from all over the world are preparing to introduce themselves by saying a few words about their own spirituality, so I begin thinking about how to express mine.

In the dream, I see that I have been defining my mature spirituality in terms of what I no longer believe, and the thought stops me short. It occurs to me that this is essentially negative. Something in me cries out that it is not enough simply to share a list of things I no longer believe. If I do this, I have nothing to bring to the table but ideas and concepts. The real questions I need to address are: What is the essence of my spiritual life? What is the ultimate ground of my being? What kind of presence do I bring to the room?

It also occurs to me that defining faith only in terms of views, ideas, and concepts indicates a person is still simply operating within a belief system, albeit a more expansive one than he or she might have embraced in the past. At some point on the spiritual path a person needs to step out of belief systems entirely, or at least recognize them as such.

Luminous Presences

So, in the dream, as all this is going through my head, and just before my turn comes to speak, I look out the window and happen to notice an old friend of mine standing outside. I rush through the door and greet him midway down the stairs. He recognizes me at once and we share a warm embrace. Then I feel an overwhelming impulse to communicate to him the essence of the revelation I have just had concerning faith as an embodiment of presence rather than a rejection or affirmation of beliefs. Almost telepathically, I share that the essence of my faith is trying to live as one who has entrusted herself entirely and fearlessly to the universe.

The name Susan, I was once told, means lily, but also trusting, a quality of the carefree "lilies of the field" of which Jesus spoke, who "neither toil nor spin." But this kind of trust isn't based on a naïve assumption that I am specially protected. It assumes that God (or whatever name we use to point to that living Presence within us and everything else) is unstoppable. And suddenly I say out loud to my friend, "It seems the time has come for those who call themselves Christians to move from the personal adoration of Jesus to the realization of the Christ-consciousness within."

In the Christian tradition the state of awakened, compassionate presence is called "having the mind of Christ." In other traditions something analogous goes by other names but they refer to a similar individual embodiment of divine love and wisdom. For a Christian, the overflow of the Christ-consciousness becomes compassionate action in the world. My dream friend seems to get it. We are of the same mind on the issue of moving beyond belief systems and living the principles we profess.

Fear Ousts Presence

I realize in the wake of the dream that my life has been filled with many hidden anxieties that have been getting in the way of my fullest potential. Of course, we need to distinguish real fears, like the presence of hostile Romans, from hidden fears of our own mental constructions that keep us from being fully present. I recognize too that fear is not unique to me but is part of the habitual human condition. It is the legacy of the fight or flight dynamic developed as a means of survival by our hunter-gatherer ancestors. Much of our collective greed, selfishness, and tendency toward self-destructiveness can be traced to this primal sense of insufficiency.

Fear leads to racism and warfare through the demonizing of the other. Fear lurks behind our anxiety that the current familiar and comfortable state of things will not last, and that we are endlessly subject to loss, harm, disease, and ultimately death.

Deep down it scares us that we can't control everything, despite our best efforts. And of course this is perfectly true. Nothing temporal lasts, so to an extent our fear is justifiable. However, the secret suggested by the passage from the Gospel of Thomas is that we have a timeless inner self that is one with the unconditioned ground of the cosmos. A part of us is eternally present, deathless, and endlessly safe. Jesus isn't talking just about himself but about each one of us when he says, "Light shines out from the centre of light and illuminates the whole cosmos."

This secret is the source of the burning light that emerges out of the darkness of uncertainty and unknowing – the light that belongs on a lampstand rather than being stuck under a bushel. This light shining in darkness is the very essence of our being.

Mystical Dreams and Other Stirrings

My Cappadocian dream, then, suggests why mysticism has drawn me so profoundly over the past decades and why I'm writing, speaking, and teaching on the mystical streams within Christianity as they intersect with those of other spiritual traditions. The mystical element in all religions involves the actualization of ever more integral, inclusive, and holistic states of being. As we allow love and compassion to be activated in our daily lives, our doctrinal and ideological attachments, though important in terms of our cultural history and development, fall away in the face of the deeper things that unite us.

When I first met my mystic mentor, Olga Park, it was not exactly what she said that moved me to study with her for sixteen years, but the quality of her presence, her being, what you could call the radiance of her soul. She shone a light that flamed not just in her words and insights, but through every particle of her. Just being around her lifted me to a higher level. In the imagery used by Jesus she was a living lamp and consequently a catalyst to my own growth.

Mystical Awareness

The more liberal forms of Christianity emphasize tolerance, ethics, reason, social justice – all essential things. However, if Christianity is to survive into the future, my dream suggests it must bring to the table an active practice of divine, universal presence in each of us, one that overflows into our communities. This is where the cultivation of mystical awareness comes in, through practices like meditation, contemplative prayer, and other ways of entering more regularly into the deep interior silences where we make ourselves available to the divine.

For me, coming into presence has come down to beginning each day with about twenty minutes of silence where I ask the Holy One to use me as She will throughout the day. Olga taught me that the first gateway on the spiritual path is humility – the desire to give ourselves over to a purpose higher than that of our own constructions. In our unevolved selves or egos we simply don't know enough or think big enough to know what to ask for. So I begin and end my daily practice with an expression of the desire to serve: Here I am, available for use.

The big question in my life has moved from my childhood's, What must I do to be saved? to my middle years' issue, How must I live in order to contribute to the common good? to more recently, How am I opening to divine Presence so that I can become a global activist, an embodiment of spiritual healing in the world? How is the Christ-light expressing itself in and through me and the network of relationships in which I find myself?

As a child in the Presbyterian Church my religious sensibility expressed itself as a desire to be good in the sense of being nice, sweet, liked, approved. Today this early piety has shifted to a desire to actually *be the good* – that is, to participate in the generous, kind, compassionate, justice-making, unselfish longings of the universe. As we mature, true goodness needs to take the place of emotional piety. To be truly good, we sometimes have to get rid of our "good girl" or "good boy" without violating a deeper morality. Faith moves from a sense that God can take care of everything to the intuitive knowledge that we have never left the divine Presence and can choose to live in it more fully and consciously.

Mysticism is a desire for intimate union with the divine that we once vaguely conceived as Other. We move from a childlike sense of feeling safe and protected by an external God who we can ask to keep us from evil to another sense of trust that assures us God is present within us in the midst of unknowing and uncertainty. The Romantic poet Keats called this state "negative capability," as good an oxymoron as I've found on mystical unknowing, that state in which a person "is capable of being in uncertainties, Mysteries, doubts, without any irritable reaching after fact & reason."[1] Keats is not denying the value of reason but pointing to the immense power that awakes in us when we open to a beauty and a mystery we cannot fathom solely with our rational minds.

Unconditional Openness

When we experience pain, loss, or suffering, God is with us in the process, giving us the grace to walk through whatever comes. We can seek to cultivate in our daily lives what Buddhist teacher Pema Chodron calls "unconditional openness."[2] This kind of receptivity is in itself a state of fearlessness. Yet even when we slip back into fear we can learn to be tender with ourselves precisely because of our fear and doubt. We can forgive ourselves and embrace our imperfections as ongoing opportunities for Spirit to manifest in our weaknesses in new ways. Sometimes making friends with our fear and abiding with it for a while is the best means of releasing it.

On Being Light-Bearers

The Gospels use the mystical symbolism of light to talk about this sense of embodying God, or being constellations and occasions of divine presence in the world.

The Gospel of Thomas is clear on how humans are meant to become centres of illumination. We are called not to worship the Christ as an external figure, but to become gushing fountains of love and creativity like him. So this urge to shine our light is presented as an imperative, for, as the words of Jesus suggest, if we are not mediating light we are mediating the darkness of our severance from the whole. Jesus didn't wish his followers to get stuck in worshipping an external image of him but to drink from the same living waters from which he drank. So it is never too late to let go of fear and enter into the palace of presence that we are. There we shall meet that fearless part of ourselves that never left the great unity, that part of us that has been present with God "from the foundations of the world."

I'd like to close with a poem I wrote when I was puzzling over why it says in the book of Revelation that the fearful may not enter the holy kingdom. At first this seemed like the prohibition of a harsh God, but as I thought about the symbolic meaning of the passage, it seemed to suggest that the state of fear itself is incompatible with love.

The Fearful Shall Not Enter

The angel's first words are always,
"Fear not, fear not."

And in the holy now kingdom
no fear mongers or anxious ones,

not because anyone is excluded,
but since fear casts us from our deepest selves.

Most of our lives a fending off of phantoms
who, if they come, are not as they seem.

How many dreams a prospect of emptying,
falling, waking out of terror?

How many deaths a passport to somewhere
unimagined?[3]

1 John Keats, "Letter to George and Tom Keats, Dec. 21–27, 1817," in *English Romantic Writers* (Ed. David Perkins; NY: Harcourt, 1967), 1209.

2 Pema Chodron, *The Places That Scare You: a Guide to Fearlessness in Difficult Times* (Boston: Shambhala, 2002), 100.

3 Susan McCaslin, *At the Mercy Seat* (Vancouver, BC: Ronsdale Press, 2003), 25.

Chapter Eight

A Warless World

The wolf shall live with the lamb,
the leopard shall lie down with the kid,
the calf and the lion and the fatling together,
and a little child shall lead them.
The cow and the bear shall graze,
Their young shall lie down together;
and the lion shall eat straw like the ox.
~ ISAIAH 11:6–7

Jesus was the most active resister known perhaps to history. This was non-violence par excellence.
~ MOHANDAS GANDHI

We Who Have Ears

listen to the sounds of war:

crack of cannonball, staccato of machine gun,
bullet's thwack between shoulders, soldier's groan

whistle of missiles, buzz of drone, stark silence
before bombs thud faceless on human faces.

open to the sounds of peace:

soft sheets of rain drawn over hydrangeas,
mother's serenade to a sleeping child

doctor's light sweep over a fevered brow,
voices lamenting the derelict rubble of war.

see what made the prophet Isaiah laugh:
fierce wolf and trembling lamb entwined.

affirm the vision of the peace-makers:
a warless world with everyone as one.

drop the curriculum of war
for new ways of studying peace.

transform our weapons of mass destruction
*into wind turbines and solar technologies for
the planet's health.*

say with the prophet Isaiah, "War no more,"
*until we "no more hurt or destroy in all our
holy mountain."*

I **am** the daughter of a World War II veteran. My dad flew transport in the Philippines and could have been shot down at any time. I'm proud of his willingness to risk his life in the war. Yet I also believe it's time to penetrate to the causes of war and put our enormous collective creative potential into non-violent solutions to conflict.

When I hit university and became an anti-war protester during the Vietnam War, my peacenik ways and Dad's patriotism collided. I moved to Canada in 1969 because of my sense that the United States was engaged in an immoral war, but my dad and I never stopped communicating. We disagreed over the bomb, the domino theory, and the actions of the draft dodgers, whom I saw as conscientious objectors and heroic war resisters. But we never lost our loving connection and Dad told me many times that though we clashed on foreign policy he respected, loved, esteemed me, and valued my idealism.

Not everyone who disagreed with the hippies was quite as tolerant of difference. Even now, peaceniks and pacifists are sometimes reviled and not taken seriously. My sense is that we have to get past seeing all peacemakers as naïve or unrealistic and look at non-violent peacemaking as the ultimate pragmatism, the only means of survival as a species. For peacemakers act out of a very visceral realization that violence not only begets more and more violence, but that the cycle is unending and unsustainable.

Non-violent activists such as Mohandas Gandhi and Martin Luther King, Jr. are people who devised effective strategies for resisting injustice without resorting to brute force. Studying their lives, I have learned it takes enormous resolve, courage, intelligence, and strength to be a peacemaker. Peacemaking is not for the weak or faint-hearted.

My aspiration is to stand with those who long to bring about peace in the world. Yet I am not an absolutely unqualified pacifist because I realize there may be times when force is needed to defend innocent people against genocide and other criminal violations of basic human rights.

Sliding into Default Position

The problem is that once anyone concedes that there are occasions when force or some form of global policing is necessary, people slide all too readily into the default position of violence without exhausting other more creative alternatives, such as diplomacy, dialogue, humanitarian aid, education, and the relief of poverty. Yet the "just war" notion that applies to the defeat of Fascism in World War II continues to be trotted out to rationalize wars that are not analogous and where violence is counterproductive for all. Given the havoc that war can inflict on all life on the planet, the term "just war" as it is usually applied is a contradiction in terms, especially for its victims.

We need, therefore, more thoughtful means of discerning when force is justified and when it is not. My suspicion is that the occasions when all-out force is required are very few. Thomas Merton argued that the use of violence should only be entered into with a sense of deep regret after all peaceful means have been exhausted. With Gandhi, he felt a non-violent approach could give us a "better chance of curing the illness instead of contracting it."[1]

Gifts of the Artists

Because my area of expertise is poetry, I have asked myself what gifts poets and artists bring to the community as peacemakers. One important thing the poet does is to create an imagination of peace. By imagination, I don't simply mean fantasy, but the creative mind within each of us. Poets can imagine ways to adapt and evolve to more refined ways of knowing and being. War is an immense failure of imagination.

As humans, we are capable of imagining alternative realities. Once we imagine a better world, we have the choice of willing transformation, first in our own lives and then in the community and global sphere. The symbols of the prophets and visionaries from our religious traditions can actually help us shift consciousness since these images and emblems arise from a deep impulse toward non-violence that counters and may even trump our primal addiction to violence. To see the higher path and carry an image of it in our hearts is to become part of that path. Getting a taste of peace can lead to a commitment to peace.

The Lion and the Wolf Within

Awaken your heart to peace. Close your eyes and imagine the beating of swords into ploughshares. Instruments of destruction become the means to grow food. Imagine men, women, and children gathering to dismantle nuclear weapons and using the materials and technology that produced them to create green technologies. Meditate on the words "they shall not learn [or study] war anymore" and think of all the scientific research and money that goes into warfare; then imagine those resources given over to transforming our social systems to serve our poorest members and reduce the gap between the haves and the have-nots.

My favourite image from the First Testament is that of the wolf lying down with the lamb and the leopard frolicking with the kid. The more familiar image of the lion resting with the lamb isn't actually in the Bible, but you get the idea. The usually aggressive predator and its prey seem to be cohabiting beautifully in what seems a utopian vision. Recently though, I've read these passages differently, seeing them as hints of what is possible now within each of us. If we take the passage literally, we end up rejecting lions and wolves, who are in fact nurturing creatures of extreme delicacy, power, and intelligence. Yet if we think of the wolf here as a symbol of the old reptilian brain in each person and the lamb the more recently developed neo-cortex – centre of imagination and higher consciousness – the picture changes. The prophet may be saying that we cannot and should not try to eliminate the magnificent wolf since the old flight-fight system is part of our evolutionary heritage. That potentially violent or predatory part of ourselves, when acknowledged, should be allowed to relax and come to the table of our collective being. What the prophet's words point to is that the old brain can be transformed to work in harmony with the new brain to create a new type of peaceful human being who is no longer the slave of his survival instincts and primordial cravings. The wolf-kid or lion-lamb person who transforms the best of both lion and lamb energies within the self just might be a peaceful activist.

We Are the Other

The saying of the just king as recorded in Jesus' parable in Matthew, "As you have done it unto the least of these you have done it to me," is much more than part of a scenario about how God will reward the blessed for their good deeds. Jesus points us to a profound law of interconnection that moves beyond them-us distinctions. We are part and parcel of one another, even those we consider to be strange, different, or our enemies.

Soldiers experience this reality of deep interconnection in a negative way when they are thrown into the killing fields. Sadly, using violence damages or psychically mutilates the inner self (what the ancients called the soul). We now call the psychic aftermath of being in a war zone post-traumatic stress disorder. As many of the young soldiers returning from Iraq and Afghanistan have discovered, such soul-damage cannot be cured by a few months of rehabilitation. A significant number of those who suffer extreme psychic trauma from war resort to suicide.

Desiring to become a peacemaker, then, is not naïve; it goes to the root of our mutuality. We are actually all one human family linked to the life of the planet, but we don't all know it yet. Peacemakers act from this profound sense of kinship with all living things.

~ ~ ~ Susan McCaslin ~ ~ ~

The Current War and the Next

Often we tend to applaud peace in the abstract, but fail to apply our creative minds rigorously to the implications of the current wars under our very noses. For instance, there hasn't been a great deal of public debate here in Canada about the war in Afghanistan, as many of us know very little about the history of conflict in that wartorn region. For a while it was assumed that with enough troops we could accomplish what Britain and Russia failed to accomplish.[2] Yet quite a few military experts and humanitarian aid workers have become critical of the war.

The war in Afghanistan is a complex one that will not be won simply by bringing in new counter-insurgency moves while naively hoping to build community. In fact, looking back at history, Afghanistan bears striking parallels to Vietnam: an occupation of a smaller nation by Western powers that is unpopular at home and involves violence against civilians. Our presence in Afghanistan has created more enemies and terrorists in the Islamic world than friends and allies. Keeping standing armies in developing nations is not sustainable for the West. Trying to rebuild infrastructures while toting machine guns and navigating smart bombs doesn't make things better for the people we say we are trying to help, or increase security in the West.

Prominent Afghan activist Malalai Joya has expressed her disappointment with military interventions in her country despite her awareness of the Taliban's mistreatment of women. Joya, formerly an elected member of the Afghan parliament, publicly denounced the presence of warlords and war criminals in the parliament and subsequently was attacked physically by her fellow parliamentarians. Joya has written a memoir critical of the war.[3] Noam Chomsky, who has commended her for her courage, notes that her work shows "we can provide a helping hand – not with landmines, bullets and bombs, but with an invasion of hospitals, clinics, and schools for boys and girls."[4]

The warnings of such thoughtful leaders about the futility of violence, coupled with the news of widespread election fraud and the West's complicity in the opium trade, increase the sense that it doesn't work to impose democracy on a society from without, especially by force. Societies generally require decades to progress through the stages of cultural development necessary for democracy to thrive. Most of the major spiritual traditions teach that true change only comes from within and cannot be imposed from without, particularly not by nations that have their own agendas and lack sensitivity to the cultures they desire to control. If we do not develop our understanding of the spiritual principles that apply to these situations, we risk perpetuating violence that only exacerbates the underlying social and political problems.

Being Peace

Whatever the complexities of this current war and the related peacekeeping efforts, peace cannot be achieved worldwide until we individually enter the state of peace in our everyday lives. So we need first to build peace within the inner self, peace in the family, peace in the local community, and peace in the global or planetary community. My father told me that the hardest lesson in life for him was to learn to love himself. That's the starting point.

What happens when we realize our intimate connection with others and step up to be peacemakers in the world? Not only do we practice loving-kindness as individuals, but in groups we become creativity units, peace think-tanks. What if even half the money spent on guns, bombs, and other weapons was given over to feeding and educating people, and supporting the arts? What if our nation truly invested heavily in defining its role as a peace-making nation, as a people whose rejection of violence intensified our innovative efforts to increase humanitarian aid and resolve international conflicts? Moving in this direction is by no means easy work, especially when dealing with other cultures that have a completely different history and way of looking at the world. It's far easier to throw our hands up and send in the drones.

War No More

It's important that we remember the past in order to learn from it. Therefore we honour our vets on Remembrance Day by mourning the grievous devastations of war, and by committing ourselves resolutely to a non-violent waging of peace in the world. Let's say with the ancient prophet Isaiah, "War no more." Let's donate our lives to Jesus' great dream of the building of the kingdom (kin-dom[5] or community) of heaven on earth. Let's make each day into peace-making day and stand with those who dedicate their lives to the vision of a warless world.

---

1   Thomas Merton, *Faith and Violence* (Notre Dame, IN: University of Notre Dame Press, 1986), 12.

2   Now that Canada is slowly withdrawing its military operations in the country, one wonders when we will be drawn into the next futile war.

3   Malalai Joya, *A Woman Among Warlords: the Extraordinary Story of an Afghan Who Dared to Speak Out* (Scribner's, 2009). Joya, Malalai. http://en.wikipedia.org/wiki/Malalai_Joya

4   Ibid

5   Rev. Bruce Sanguin, author of *Darwin, Divinity, and the Dance of the Cosmos* (WoodLake Books), often uses the term "kin-dom" instead of "kingdom" to replace the word's usual authoritarian connotations with the sense of an order governed by spiritual kinship and respect.

Chapter Nine

Blessed

*Blessed are the poor in spirit,
for theirs is the kingdom of heaven.*

~ MATTHEW 5:3

*I love Jesus, who said to us:
Heaven and earth will pass away.
When heaven and earth have passed away,
my word will remain.
What was your word, Jesus?
Love? Affection? Forgiveness?
All your words were
one word: Wakeup.*

~ ANTONIO MACHADO,
FROM MORAL PROVERBS AND FOLK SONGS,
TRANS. ROBERT BLY

Creative Spirit,

Listen to the wisdom of Jesus

*who taught us that to be poor is to be rich,
to grieve is to be comforted,
to be meek is to be bold,
to hunger and thirst for alignment is to be full*

*to be merciful is to swim in an ocean of mercy,
to make peace is to be at peace with self
    and others,
to love justice is to affirm our home in the earth,
to struggle without knowing outcomes is
    to live into being.*

*Help us to live these explosions of light,
these spice boxes of paradox,
these mind-boggling koans,
these radical riffs*

that are your Beatitudes

*so we may transcend duality
and set up housekeeping
in your household of peace.*

The resounding note of the Beatitudes is the word *blessed.*

To be blessed is to be deeply grounded in what the 13th-century mystic Mechthild of Magdeburg called the flowing light of the Godhead. Mechthild's Godhead is creative energy, intelligence, and compassion, a presence that lives in all things and in which all have their being. The primary thing about this energy is that it flows.

The Taoists call a similar vital power the Te, which is difficult to translate because it means so much more than just natural virtue or goodness. It's a life force, a blessedness that is our original birthright, a state of unconditioned consciousness in which we are profoundly cherished. By removing impediments to this original condition, such as our socialization, narrow mental constructs, and fears, we return in deep rejoicing to our home within that which is. That's why being blessed goes hand in hand with joy and a sense of abundance.

Neil Douglas-Klotz, a scholar of Aramaic (the vernacular language that Jesus spoke), provides another translation of this first beatitude: "Ripe are those who reside in breath; to them belongs the reign of unity. Or, blessed are those who realize that breath is their first and last possession, theirs is the 'I Can' of the cosmos."[1] In other words, the so-called poor in spirit are those who breathe in harmony with the breath of God, realizing that breath is all they truly own.

By centring on the poverty of apparent emptiness, we poise ourselves for action, since all acts emanate from the eternal silence within. The Greek word *makairos* is a passive form meaning "supremely blessed," "fortunate," "well off," or "happy." However, in Aramaic the phrase is active and means something more like "wake up" or "get up," which resonates with Antonio Machado's proposition that Jesus was calling those around him to awaken to more than personal salvation. The import of the message becomes, get up you who are poor in spirit; or even, awakened are the poor in spirit. Jesus is calling us to incarnate this divine breath in the world.[2] It's a prophetic wake-up call, or what the East would call enlightenment.

Holy Poverty

For Jesus, to be poor in spirit is not to lack Spirit-power or to be dis-spirited, but rather to experience loss or poverty as something we share with God. For God is the emptiness as well as the fullness. God, or the eternal consciousness that dwells within yet transcends all, is the One who suffers most intensely with us and in us when we suffer. Yet this Presence constantly enacts a trajectory toward joy. So to be poor in spirit is to have entered into what mystics call the *via negativa* or divine darkness. This stage of spiritual growth is what an anonymous 14th-century English priest called the "cloud of unknowing." When we enter that cloud, we don't know the outcome of our suffering, and are not given definitive answers to the problem of pain and suffering or the apparent absence of God. Yet absence can be a form of Presence.

The Beatitudes illustrate that Jesus is a master of oxymoron, the kind of bull's eye paradox that takes apparent opposites and allows them to explode into non-dual knowing, or what the mystics call unitive being. To live this particular beatitude, not just understand it, one needs to bring together the words blessed and poor. This is a hard thing to do in a materialistic culture.

St. Francis of Assisi, who embraced the metaphor of wedding Lady Poverty and who renounced wealth, understood that to be poor in spirit with a small s is to be rich in Spirit with a capital S. Often, the poor in material things are freer from attachments and obsessions with things, their maintenance and upkeep, than their more materially comfortable brothers and sisters. But holy poverty is not the grinding poverty of those victimized by an unjust system. This saying should never be used to justify society's failure to relieve the suffering of its poorest members. Poverty of spirit is the poverty of the everyday saint, mystic, mother, father, worker, teacher, or student who comes into the Presence with empty hands, a quieted mind, and a receptive heart, letting go of ego agendas and a conventional sense of rightness.

The poor in spirit move toward an emptying of themselves. And because they are not so attached to their self-definitions and ego constructions they are free to serve others. The New Testament calls this process kenosis, and speaks of the kenotic Christ as one who "emptied himself." The poor are those who have found out, painfully perhaps, that the more spiritually mature we are, the less we know. Socrates, for instance, when asked about why the Delphic oracle had called him the wisest of men, discovered it was because he alone knew he knew nothing. In other words, he was poor in spirit.

Emily Dickinson wrote a poem demonstrating the mystic way most aptly:

> I'm nobody, who are you?
> Are you nobody, too?
> Then there's a pair of us – don't tell!
> They'd banish us, you know!
>
> How dreary to be somebody!
> How public like a frog
> To tell one's name the livelong day
> To an admiring bog!

So poverty of Spirit is a form of humility. It is the wisdom of those who receive inspiration from the deep within because they are not filled up with their own knowing. It's the posture of those bereft of ready answers, tidy maps, and closed-system thinking. It's the position of those stripped down to what Shakespeare called "poor unaccommodated man." These will not just inherit the kingdom; they *are* the kingdom of heaven on earth. They incarnate it in their lives of receptivity to Holy Oneness.

The Staggering Beauty of the Beatitudes

Many of the Jesus historians conclude that the pithy, enigmatic Beatitudes are authentic, even though they probably were not delivered all at the same time. I think they are among Jesus' essential teachings, replicating the rhythms and cadences of his speech.

When I ponder the Beatitudes, I'm always bowled over by their deceptive simplicity, teasing paradoxes, heart-rending power, and infinite disclosures of meaning. They parallel the koans, or paradoxical sayings of Zen Buddhism that are designed to push the mind of the seeker to enlightenment. Jesus' sayings have the same radical, going-to-the-root-of-things quality. They baffle our customary concepts of how the world works and use humour and shock to overturn conventional assumptions. "Blessed are the meek, for they shall inherit the earth." Huh? One's first reaction is usually, "Well, maybe this is how things work in utopia, but not on this planet!" Yet to abandon the saying at this point is to miss the opportunity for deeper openings.

"Let us go in deeper and speak more openly," says the mystic Hugh of St. Victor. And this is exactly what these little cosmic teasers force us to do. Maybe the meek, then, are not just those who are weak or disempowered, but people who are able to be still and feel their connection to the earth. They inherit the earth because they have rejoined the spiritual powers that work with, not against, the Gaia impulses of peace and justice. The earth is theirs because they are one with it, not because they own it.

In addition, people have been tempted to see these sayings as predictions of a time in the future or in heaven when there will be a great reversal: those at the bottom of the domination hierarchies will be on top and vice versa. If the universe is "fair," they believe, then evildoers will get their just deserts. Although we hope there will be ultimate justice, Jesus' other teachings are not about an inversion of the power system but the emergence of a spiritual realm or community where no one is the loser.

The universe, as much as it seems like a survival of the fittest game, may in the end be a sum-sum, win-win act of balancing and regeneration through mutuality and love.

A Few New Beatitudes

Blessedness can reside in relinquishing some of the things we think we most need to ensure our happiness. When the emergent cosmos seems to deny us the things we most desire, we can choose to enter a state of gratitude for the tremendous gifts hidden in apparent loss. Recently, I've written a few new Beatitudes.

> Blessed are you who are overlooked for the
> Governor General's Award, for yours is the white
> fire of the creative forge.
> Blessed are you who have no swimming pool,
> for yours is the freedom from cleaning autumn
> leaves out of the ducts.
> Blessed are you who have been marginalized,
> for yours are the liminal spaces.

Liminality in that last line refers to the places between, the worlds neither here nor there. It's the place where magic happens – a borderless condition of immense freedom.

Often, before insight on a particular Jesus saying flows in, there is a process of letting go of previous ideas. Well, if he didn't mean that, then what was he getting at? And there is never a final answer. As many times as I have meditated on these poetic, parallel-structured couplets, I've never reached the end of a single one. I can go on explicating and analyzing if I want, but my net of concepts just can't hold more than a fraction of the wisdom. Sometimes, however, when I experience the essence of the saying directly, it penetrates what the mystics call the eye of the heart.

The important thing about this process of meditation is that after my mental-emotional lingering with the words finishes, and after my "pen has gleaned by teeming brain," as Keats put it, I am returned to silence. And then, sometimes, the koan rises before me afresh in all its mystery, beauty, and simplicity. All efforts to break it down, figure it out, lie in shards.

And in that I am blessed, not because I got it or didn't get it, but because of the process.

Meditating with the Beatitudes

There is a time to remain in silence, and a time to let language speak. "Thought and speech are the organic vehicles of Holy Spirit," said my spiritual mentor Olga Park. By meditating on the words of Jesus we may enter the living structures of his imagination, because his words are timeless. People called Jesus master, rabbi, and teacher for a reason: he had mastered wisdom teaching. His aphorisms sprang from the most integral level. Meditation on sacred scripture (*lectio divina*) is not a mere intellectual exercise but a graced plunge into transformation.

Of course, not all the words attributed to Jesus in scripture are necessarily his, since the Gospel writers framed, interpreted, and elaborated on his life in order to speak to their particular communities. The Bible is intensively edited. It is constructed by humans, not handed down verbatim from above. Nevertheless, we can test the words attributed to Jesus for their innate authenticity. In doing so, there can be an at-one-ment of our mind with the mind of Christ-wisdom. The Christ-mind within us is a living teacher. We can come into communion by relinquishing our usual thought patterns and entering the kingdom of Jesus' images and symbols. In this sense, his words become Spirit, bread of heaven, and life, as the Gospel of John states: "The Words that I have spoken to you are spirit and life" (John 6:63).

Meek but Not Weak

What is it to be truly meek? Is humble a better translation? Perhaps gentle? Meditating on Jesus' words is a process of discarding and taking up possibilities till the mind exhausts itself. At some point (and getting to it can take a few seconds, hours, or days), something shifts, and something unexpected flows in that is your own thought and not your thought. You open to newness from within. Sometimes inspiration falls into your soul like manna. Whatever metaphor you use, there is a divine "Aha!" and a quiet release of breath.

However, not every meditation on the words of Jesus will yield such fruit. The danger is in striving too hard. Although the process of meditation is active, it involves quieting the discursive intellect and opening to creative mind. Meditation that begins as an active engagement with a sacred text can become a form of opening to the silence. Eventually, in what have been called the deeper states of contemplation, one is content to sink into the profound silence of sheer being where it is better to *be* than to know. Contemplation of this sort is a clearing of a sacred space or temple of the self.

There are various movements of Spirit in us and it is not for us to control them or try to define them too precisely. When entering these deeper levels of union, our texts and limited interpretations fall away and we linger in the presence of the Holy One. Yet both meditating on and contemplating in at-one-ment are treasures hidden in the field of our awareness. Engraving just one of these radical, iconic beatitudes on the scroll of our hearts invites the others in, and as we begin to incarnate them, to live them, we are blessed.

---

1 Neil Douglas-Klotz, *The Hidden Gospel: Decoding the Spiritual Message of the Aramaic Jesus* (Wheaton Illinois: Quest Books, 1999), 41.

2 Charles R. Page, *Jerusalem Institute of Biblical Exploration.* http://www.jibe-edu.org/clientImages/28237/JCJournalArticles/thebeatitudes.pdf

Chapter Ten

Peaceful Resisters

But I say to you that listen, Love your enemies, do good to those who hate you, bless those who curse you, pray for those who abuse you.

~ LUKE 6:27–28

Spirit of Peace and Reconciliation,

When the saints come marching in

let's have them galloping, skipping, bounding,
let's have them rung in with tympani or sung
   with bel canto
or dancing like ladies or leaping lords.

Let's have them chanting om or halleluiah,
feasted or fasted, lumbering or still,
or creeping in like fog on "little cat feet."

Rough golden codgers or slick newborns dropped,
trailing clouds of gaiety, or glory,
amazing themselves that there are so many ways to be.

Let's have them ululating or rumbaing,
shaking their glorious boodies,
gleefully naked or clad in gold tissue

but please, please, don't let them be marching,
marching, marching, goose-stepping and proud
as to jihad, crusade, or war.

Human nature is drenched in the bloodstains of violence. But is this deeply embedded aggressiveness ineradicable? Are the bulk of humans, as Jonathan Swift put it, "the most pernicious race of odious vermin that nature ever suffered to crawl upon the surface of the earth"?[1] Psychologist James Hillman argues that, whatever else is true, humans are deeply addicted to violence, that the god Mars is still alive and well in the human psyche, and that to ignore our deep attraction to him is to remain in denial.[2] He delineates our war-like pride and its alliance with belligerent religion as our most salient feature from earliest times.

However, if we consider the examples of many spiritual mentors, mystics, and teachers throughout the ages, we discover there is another figure within that has scarcely shown its face on the social-political stage – that of the peaceful *anthropos* or spiritual human being. In the Gospels, the visions of the ancient Hebrew prophets Daniel and Ezekiel, and the writings of some of the Gnostics, this figure is called the Son of Man, a term that can be translated as "offspring of the human," "the one like the person,"[3] or the "emergent human being."[4]

In his studies on violence,[5] philosopher René Girard explores the primal roots of human conflict, pointing out that people discovered how a community's scapegoating of a designated victim brought about a temporary peace-inducing awe, a brief dispersal of the violence, and a continuation of the cycle. He argues that Jesus' death exposed the futility of the scapegoat mechanism. The point is that violence as a deterrent to more violence hasn't really worked. And given the capacity of humans to destroy themselves as a species, it is now evident that violence is not a tenable or effective means of bringing about peace, or indeed, of being together on the planet.

What Lies Deepest within Us?

My analysis of the roots of violence diverges from that of Hillman, for although the image of the "beast" or self-serving, violent human resides within us, so does that of the spiritual *anthropos*, or child of divine creativity and compassion. The question is not a choice between whether humans are basically evil creatures whose lives are "nasty, brutish, and short," as the philosopher Hobbes believed, or whether we are basically good, like Rousseau's noble savage. Humans are not fundamentally one or the other, but have the capacity for all kinds of admixtures of characteristics. The proper question, then, is: What we are to become? Another way to put it is: How do we want to be in the present so as to shape positively what we are to be? And that is an open-ended question that assumes some degree of freedom of choice, individually and collectively.

War Resisters

The issue of what we are to become is relevant to the question about whether Iraq war resisters should be allowed to remain in Canada. Some argue that the situation with the "defectors" isn't analogous to that of the Vietnam era because the soldiers weren't drafted but signed up voluntarily for the war and knew what they were getting into. They are seen by some as cowards who are breaking their contracts. However, many of the recruits were misled or lied to about the morality of the activities in which they would be engaged, or were victims of economic pressure to join up. The picture altered for them when they experienced first-hand that the Iraq war not only involved massive human rights abuses, but was also illegal according to international law. That people evolve morally and spiritually has to be taken into account. These young dissenters have become peaceful *anthropoi* who should have the right of conscientious objection.

Artists, psychologists, philosophers, and theologians continue to analyze the dynamics of violence and its roots in fear and greed, and to seek ways to stop the spiralling cycle. It has often been acknowledged that if humans cannot transcend their violent streak they will die out as a species. Evolve or die, the saying goes. Since the development of the atomic bomb, writers such as Thomas Merton have asserted that warfare as a means of resolving disputes needs to become obsolete.

Religion and Violence

History reveals that many religious institutions, out of fear and the desire to maintain power, have become perpetrators of violence, as illustrated in Christianity by the Crusades and the Inquisition. Yet this type of Christianism is not at all what Jesus taught. Jesus emphasized forgiveness, tolerance, and love of one's enemy. He taught that God is love and not to be feared: a loving father, one he called *Abba,* an affectionate term meaning something like "Daddy."

Studying the teachings and lives of the founders of the world's religions (including Christianity) brings an alternative vision to the issue of violence. The Buddha, for instance, taught loving compassion for all sentient beings. We need to ask what our various spiritual teachers have to say about how to be instruments of peace in the world.

Jesus and Non-Violence

In the case of Jesus, what stands out is his complete, unabashed commitment to non-violence. He refuses to retaliate in the face of the forces of Empire that are threatened by him. He chooses not to react with violence to the violence that is done to him and instructs his followers to put away their swords when he is arrested in the garden. He forgives his enemies from the cross, and has compassion for them in their ignorance. The violence stops with him. Even when he expresses outrage in the temple, overturning the tables of the moneychangers, his is a symbolic act of peaceful resistance that flows from a place of unity with the one he calls Father.

Though some may feel uncomfortable with the image of a tortured, crucified figure on a cross, we need to recognize that Jesus was not a victim. Jesus died because of the reaction of the power structures of his day to his radical acts and teachings. He was perceived as a potential insurrectionist by Rome and by the authorities of the temple system who were complicit with Roman occupation. But by "setting his face steadily toward Jerusalem" and confronting the Roman seat of power, he *deliberately* placed himself in the way of the Roman crucifixion machine that dealt brutally with troublemakers.

Jesus' radical non-violence has to be brought together with his teaching on divinization (how to become what we already are – divine) so that we don't end up with a passive version of non-violence. Jesus' God is the active, evolutionary power of non-violent, non-punishing, non-retaliatory, emergent *agape* love embedded into the cosmos from its very beginning. Therefore, since this kind of love lies at the root of our being, it is time to get on with the works of peace. To move toward divinization is to open to a place where the innermost centre of the human intersects with the innermost of the cosmological divine. We and the divine within us can then become conjoined outpourings of peace, love, and creativity. Despite our capacity for violence, we also carry within us the seeds of non-violence and compassion.

Love your enemies is as radical today as it was in ancient Galilee. Most political leaders who embrace conventional forms of Christianity ignore this saying because they consider it impracticable. The problem is that although peacemaking has been exemplified in the lives of our spiritual forerunners, it has not been lived out on a large scale on the socio-political-economic plane. Jesus' way, and the way of peace in the major religions, is still pretty much an untried experiment.

Imagining Peace

Social analysts have noted that whenever there is a gang shooting, violence spreads like a virus. Dr. Gary Slukin, an epidemiologist from Chicago, has applied a concept called CeaseFire as a way to intervene in this cycle. Former gang members who have become disillusioned with violence are paid and trained to patrol neighbourhoods and move in as interrupters of retaliatory acts.[6] For instance, when someone is shot through a gang act, the peacemakers go to their hospital room or spend time with the victim's relative or friend who might be considering retaliation. Because they are part of the community and because they have renounced violence themselves, these former gang members are much more effective peacemakers than police officers who try to do the same thing.

What if this kind of intervention were enacted on a global scale? What if disillusioned soldiers who have seen first-hand the horror and futility of war were sent to be interrupters, warriors of peace, to bring about healing and reconciliation? What if in every part of the world where the urge to retaliate showed up, people arrived to intervene and stop the cycle through peaceful protests? Of course, such intervention isn't the whole answer to the problem of retaliatory violence, but it would be a beginning.

I did my Ph.D. dissertation on the little-known Welsh Christian metaphysical poet Vernon Watkins, who wrote these memorable lines in his poem "Injustice and Praise":

When the unjust, uncivil
Or brutal act wrongs
A man, and he can call
No judge to answer the throng's
Bestial hate, then
Not to retaliate
Against wicked men
Becomes him and his fate.

If in the ritual
Of vengeance he live,
He makes perpetual
His failure to forgive.[7]

Two 20th-century figures consciously enacted in their lives Jesus' teachings on non-violence: Mohandas Gandhi and Martin Luther King. Yet their experiments have not been embraced widely enough. Spiritual communities like those of the Quakers and the Mennonites have also taken up non-violence in a serious way. Such groups and individuals offer foretastes of what the world would look like if more of us became non-violent resisters of injustice, transforming presences for peace.

What we need today are non-violent peace coaches and teachers to help us implement non-violence in every aspect of our lives, from the personal to the municipal to the national to the transnational levels. Our forerunners have done their jobs – so now it is time for ordinary-extraordinary people to embrace non-violence on a global scale, however complex and difficult such a task might be. It is important to know that it is possible for humanity to choose to become the peaceful one, the human-divine.

If a critical mass of people begins to live from an awareness of how profoundly interconnected we are with our fellow humans, other-than-humans, and with the planet itself, peacemaking could become an unstoppable progression. For the "peace that surpasses all understanding" is after all much more glamorous, exciting, and extravagantly heady than war. As Leonard Cohen puts it, "Love's the only engine of survival."[8]

1. Jonathan Swift, *Gulliver's Travels*, "A Voyage to Brobdingnag" (Harmondsworth, Middlesex: Penguin, 1987), 173.

2. James Hillman, *A Terrible Love of War* (New York: Penguin, 2004). Hillman writes: "In short, unless we imagine war as inhuman in the transcendent sense, inhuman as the autonomy and livingness of a divine power, war as a god, our secular models cannot imagine and cannot understand. Now we can see that war's inhumanity derives from war's autonomy and that this autonomy reveals war's nature as a mythic enactment explaining both its bloodletting as ritual sacrifice, and its immortality – that it can never be laid to rest" (77).

3. Bruce Chilton, *Rabbi Jesus: an Intimate Biography* (New York: Doubleday, 2000). Chilton argues that Jesus drew on the Hebrew mystical tradition of *merkabah* or "throne mysticism" through the prophets Ezekiel and Daniel for his sense of this angelic figure, often translated as "Son of Man," but more accurately, "the one like the person" (157).

4. Elaine Pagels, *The Gnostic Gospels* (New York: Vintage Books, 1989), 122–123. "The Gnostic Valentinus taught that humanity itself manifests the divine life and divine revelation....Valentinus did not use the term in its contemporary sense, to refer to the human race taken collectively. Instead, he and his followers thought of Anthropos (here translated 'humanity') as the underlying nature of that collective entity, the archetype, or spiritual essence, of human being" (122).

5. René Girard, *Violence and the Sacred*. (Trans. Patrick Gregory; Baltimore: the Johns Hopkins University Press), 1977.

6. Miro Cernetig, "Violence as an Infectious Disease," *The Vancouver Sun*. (9 May 2008): A2.

7. Vernon Watkins, *The Collected Poems of Vernon Watkins* (Ipswich, Suffolk: Golgonooza Press, 1986), 377.

8. Leonard Cohen, "The Future" from *The Future* (Sony, 1992).

Chapter Eleven

Fire on Fire

And suddenly from heaven there came a sound like the rush of a violent wind...divided tongues, as of fire, appeared among them, and a tongue rested on each of them.

~ ACTS 2:2–3

Prayer of Opening to an Evolutionary Pentecost

*Fifty days after the Passover in Egypt
a wild wind burned through Moses
    on the mountain,
singing in his cells the beauty of cosmic law:
    all barriers fell.*

Come, new Pentecostal fire, flame in us now.

*Let us celebrate the Fire Sermon of
the Buddha, the joyous surrender of Mohammed,
the intoxicating wine of Spirit that made
    Rumi so ecstatic,
the dance of the Christ before whom
    all barriers fall.*

Come, new Pentecostal fire, flame in us now.

*Burn through our narrow ideologies and beliefs.
Open us to the transforming love that moves
  the cosmos,
that blazes in the earth our mother and
  all her creatures
and before whom all barriers fall.*

Come, new Pentecostal fire, flame in us now
bringing a Pentecost of peace and
  reconciliation –
a unity in diversity – diversity in unity:
  from one source, many tongues.

As a young Presbyterian in a rather staid congregation, my impression of Pentecost was of a supernatural event where the early disciples began speaking in tongues as a sign of the descent of the Holy Spirit. I never gave the story much thought since I assumed such things no longer occurred and therefore were pretty much irrelevant to my daily life.

Fiery Tongues

My husband Mark, on the other hand, attended a Pentecostal church until he was twelve. He witnessed the charismatic phenomenon called *glossolalia,* or "speaking in tongues." Members of the congregation would lift their arms and burst out in what seemed to him highly emotional but incomprehensible babble. A person was not considered to have truly received the Holy Spirit if she had not received the gift of tongues. But it all seemed so contrived to him: when pressured by summer camp counsellors at the age of twelve, he found he could make the same strange utterances as the adults in church. Were the sounds genuine or was he making them up? When he later switched to a Baptist church, the pastor told him to "test the spirits," since what Pentecostals called the gift of tongues might be in fact be an unwanted visitation from the Devil.

The original Pentecost must have been a stupendous event, since it launched the Jesus movement and Christianity itself, a religion that has lasted over 2000 years. I would like to recast the story of Pentecost as a living parable for an evolutionary emergence of Spirit for the 21st century. So let's ask ourselves what this story might mean now.

The Jewish Roots of Pentecost

To understand the symbolic significance of this event, it helps to understand that the Christian Pentecost emerged out of the Jewish *Hag Shabu'ot* (Shavuot) or the "feast of weeks." This celebration, set fifty days after Passover (the Greek word *Pentecost* meaning "fifty days"), was observed at the time of Jesus (and long before by Israel) to celebrate a renewal of the covenant of the Law given to Moses on Mount Sinai fifty days after the first Passover in Egypt. It was also linked to an older agricultural festival where worshippers donated to God the first fruits of the harvest. Interestingly, Pentecost and Shabu'ot are associated in both traditions with earth-wisdom permeating a community through the mediation of a spiritual leader. For Judaism, this spiritual leader was Moses, but for the early church it was Jesus, their new Moses. In other words, developing Christianity transformed the Jewish Shabu'ot into Pentecost as Christians know it.

In mystical Judaism, fire signifies the spiritual realm, the power of the nameless and unnamable Holy One of Israel, and the transforming power of the divine word that came to the prophets. The seraphim are angelic beings of divine fire. When the prophet Isaiah is taken up to God's throne, an angel places a burning coal on his tongue to purify his organs of speech and enable him to prophesy. Fire also represents the eternal consciousness that burns up our small egotisms and transforms them into the holy in many spiritual traditions.

Notice too that in Acts, Luke cites the ancient Hebrew prophet Joel about the Spirit of God descending through unexpected channels, such as children, women, the very young, the very old, and even slaves:

> I will pour out my Spirit upon all flesh,
> and your sons and your daughters shall prophesy,
> and your young men shall see visions,
> and your old men shall dream dreams.
> Even upon my slaves, both men and women,
> in those days I will pour out my Spirit;
> and they shall prophesy.
>
> ~ *ACTS 2:17–18*

The early Christians associated Pentecost with the ecstatic and with things having to do with the "end times" or end of a cycle. It is linked to the coming of mystical awareness upon ordinary people and with ultimate disclosures of a universal Spirit poured out for all. Biblical scholar John Shelby Spong speaks of how the primary sign of Pentecost is that "all human barriers...fall in the power of the divine spirit."[1]

In Christian liturgies the Pentecost story has been linked to the amazing First Testament image of the raising of piles of seemingly ossified skeletons in Ezekiel's vision of the valley of dry bones. For me as a child, the parable of the enlivened bones was a rather creepy spiritual, and a puzzling lesson in anatomy complete with skeletons dancing around that went:

> The hip bone's connected to the thigh bone,
> the thigh bone's connected to the knee bone,
> the knee bone's connected to the ankle bone,
> now hear the word of the Lord.

Later I came to see the vision as a symbol for spiritual regeneration – life out of death. The early Christian movement believed that just as God promised that the nation of Israel would arise and regenerate, so God was creating a new thing through Jesus and his followers. The death of their teacher would not destroy them, but they too would rise up in a phoenix of a movement.

A Phoenix of a Movement

The early Christian Pentecost event was the unifying mystical experience of proto-Christianity, the communities that eventually emerged to become the established church. It was an event that revealed the wisdom that shone through Jesus as universal rather than merely tribal, since it spoke to all in various languages. The transformation was a collective visionary experience.

From earliest times, Christians have associated Pentecost with the birth of the *ecclesia* or church, and seen it as a baptism of the community. We have to remind ourselves that at the time of the first Pentecost the institutional Christian church as we know it did not exist, so the event is about a small community of mostly Jewish Christians in Jerusalem who were experiencing the universality of the teachings of their Lord and offering them to the world.

Eventually, trumpet, breath, wind, tongues of fire, and new wine became part of the iconography of Christendom and the event was interpreted as a fulfillment of the prediction in the Gospel of John that Jesus would send the Holy Spirit or Comforter upon his disciples after he went away. It reinforced Paul's extension of the revelation through Jesus to the Gentiles, since those who witnessed the miracle were from all parts of the Roman Empire and beyond. For the early mystical theologian Gregory of Nazianzus, Pentecost undoes Babel or the confusion of tongues recorded in Genesis and creates a universal language of spiritual unity.[2]

According to the story, not everyone witnessing the event agreed that this was a revelation of Spirit. Some thought the early morning revellers had had too much to drink. The little quip from Peter about how these people must be intoxicated at 9 a.m. on Spirit, not "liquid spirits," reminds me of the mystical symbolism of drunkenness in the poetry of Rumi, where the lover becomes drunk on the wine of Allah, the Beloved. From the author of the Song of Songs, to Rumi, to Leonard Cohen, wine and drunkenness symbolize divine intoxication. Many of the early Christians were mystics on fire because of their direct experience. After centuries of theological doctrine and dispute, we tend to forget that Christianity is at base a mystical religion.

Can Old Bones Rise?

Can the old bones of our various religious traditions undergo spiritual renewal and transformation? Only if they move to new paradigms and openings. Another way of framing this question for Christians is to ask if the dead bones of institutional Christianity can become relevant to society again, or has Christianity had its day? The latter is so only if we fail to awaken to a global and universal mystical form of Christianity that opens itself to inter-spirituality, not just ecumenicalism or dialogue among the various denominations and Christian churches.

I would like to propose we gather up old and new to celebrate an evolutionary Pentecost, a new Pentecost with much wider implications than the old, one that includes not only a diversity of religions but the earth and the entire planetary community.

What would an evolutionary Pentecost look like? I think it would have to be an integral mysticism of ecstasy and joy. The event of Pentecost in Acts is essentially a symbol of unity in diversity and diversity in unity, a mystical union where separate tongues and articulations of the divine don't divide people but are understood to come from a common source. Reading the story in this way is rather different than interpreting it as the coming of the Holy Spirit exclusively to the Christian church. The time is past for announcing Christianity to the world or proclaiming its superiority over other faiths. The time has come to place it among the various spiritual revelations of the planet, to see how it is unique and what it looks like in relation to all the other revelations of Spirit.

Can a new Pentecostal awareness permeate the structures and birth a transforming vision? Can these dead bones rise? I believe so, but individually and collectively there will have to be much shedding of exclusivist and tribal thinking. The answer is yes if we let go of attachment to dogmas, creeds, and insistence on faith as the affirmation of beliefs about Jesus. The answer is yes if we embody in our lives the universal, cosmic Christ while honouring the revelations of other spiritual traditions. Doing so doesn't involve watering down the uniqueness of the revelation that poured through Jesus of Nazareth or embracing a naïve syncretism. In a new Pentecost, there are many tongues, many ways of expressing God or the One, but all are rooted in ultimate reality and our common human condition. What will not arise is the Church as we have known it.

An evolutionary Pentecost would be global, inter-spiritual, inter-species, tolerant, inclusive, and non-dual. The Christ energy is a universal power and presence of burning, leaping, dancing, incarnate love. An evolutionary Pentecost would take into account our interconnection with all beings and with this beautiful and fragile planet. It would be a universal feast of fiery love flaming for all, a celebration of creativity that doesn't deny the uniqueness of the various paths but cherishes each one as a jewel in a single crown.

A new Pentecostal community would overcome the fear that opening to difference will entail losing something precious. In fact, what is lost is often merely ideological; the essence of spirituality – mercy, compassion, and love – is never lost. Rather than merely agreeing to disagree, we could focus on agreeing to agree on the experiential and let belief and dogmas "take their place with grace."

Rather than talking about the Buddha versus Christ, we need, like Vietnamese monk and poet Thich Nhat Hanh, to bring together *Living Buddha and Living Christ.* In Yann Martel's novel *Life of Pi,* the protagonist Pi relates how in his youth he embraced simultaneously Hinduism, Christianity, and Islam. When confronted with the apparent contradiction of his practice, he states, "I just want to love God."[3]

It isn't that we can't debate or disagree on spiritual matters, but that we need to discover a place of wisdom where disagreements stand stunned before the direct experience of the divine. Our traditions have to be sufficient containments to preserve their singularity but sufficiently open to allow creative Spirit in, again and again.

---

1 John Shelby Spong, *Rescuing the Bible from Fundamentalism* (NY: HarperSanFrancisco, 1992), 183.

2 Gregory of Nazianzus, *Oratio,* 41.16, cited in *A Dictionary of Biblical Tradition in English Literature* (Ed. David Lyle Jeffrey; Grand Rapids, Michigan: William B. Eerdmans, 1992), 597.

3 Yann Martel, *Life of Pi* (Knopf Canada, 2001), 76.

Chapter Twelve

Opening to Mystery

Then Jesus laid his hands on his [the blind man's] eyes again; and he looked intently and his sight was restored, and he saw everything clearly.

~ MARK 8:25

Presence of Possibilities,

*let the hinges of our hearts swing open
    to things we can't explain —
the unexpected remission of a stubborn cancer*

*birth of a child when conception is deemed
    "impossible,"
release from a longstanding addiction,
a moment of reunion with a loved one
    long deceased.*

*Let's not demand or expect mystical graces,
or cling to the hope of them,
or be disappointed if they don't happen.*

*Let's acknowledge there are mysteries
beyond our knowing, unaccountable
magic in the neurons and cells.*

*Help us experience daily
the astonishing in the apparently ordinary –
laugh of a crow pirouetting in space*

*a peach gladiola blooming beyond its term,
a slug who travels six inches in two hours
to its longed for haven in the grass*

*until the kingdom of heaven is spread out
    before us,
and the glory flames forth in our unrepeatable
    uniqueness.*

When it comes to the possibility of the miraculous, I locate myself in the school suggested by Hamlet's phrase, "There are more things in heaven and earth, Horatio, than are dreamt of in thy philosophy." My theology has moved steadily over the years from a somewhat naïve literalism (i.e., Jesus unquestionably multiplied loaves and fishes and walked on water) to a more symbolic approach that assumes many of these incidents are symbols for the transformative power of the wisdom teacher the early church recognized as the Christ. Yet I keep open the possibility that the literal and the metaphoric can be strangely and happily wed. That is, maybe Jesus really did miraculous healings, and the healings are symbolic as well. Perhaps he healed the blind man's physical *and* spiritual sight.

In my own spiritual journey, I have come to a place of greater openness to mystery, and have embraced a healthy unknowing that does not easily dismiss what at first seems opaque to reason and scientific rationalism. For me, a supernatural event is one our current scientific understanding does not yet have the means to explain, something that lies beyond the powers of discursive reason and empiricism to affirm or deny. However, neither do I assume all supernatural or even paranormal events are evidence of God or of Spirit acting in the world.

The term "supernatural," in the sense of a realm beyond or above the natural one, has often been used by orthodoxy to affirm a God who is of a completely different order of being than the rest of creation. This assumption can set up a two-storied universe, rather than a universe where there is one reality, one life manifesting in astonishing diversity. Mystical theologian Bruce Sanguin prefers the term "supranatural" to describe events and experiences that are "infinitely more than we can imagine, and yet not ontologically of a different order."[1] For me, a supranatural event, then, transcends but includes natural processes, sustaining them within a larger context. Mystical understanding in many traditions affirms one universe with many dimensions cohering within it.

I continue to examine each biblical incident that seems steeped in what seems supranatural in the above sense in order to consider if it could be literal, symbolic, or both. For example, I have had trouble with the virgin birth for many years, as it seems unnecessary for God to circumvent the natural birth process and the female body. The related doctrine of the immaculate conception seems to suggest human sexuality is unclean or sinful, and that Jesus was not fully human since he had to issue from a super-celestial gene pool in the sky. Besides, as scholars point out, in the phrase from Isaiah, "a *virgin* shall conceive," *virgin* in Hebrew actually means, "a young woman." However, the symbolism of virginity as an inner purity or wholeness still speaks to me deeply.

Often scriptures take on profound meaning once mystical symbols are interpreted as such. For instance, what if the virgins in the parable about the women awaiting the bridegroom's return represent not faithful believers, but people of all kinds who have opened themselves to the anointing of a deeper, more integral consciousness?

Likewise, though conservative Christians may say I have stepped outside the "fundamentals" of the faith, I question the literalness of the physical resurrection of Jesus. I am not just reacting to the scientific unlikelihood of the restoration of a dead corpse, but have to ask myself why the physical resurrection seems to be a one-off event rather than something inherent to our common humanity. Then I began to ask, what difference would it make to my faith if I should discover that Christ did not literally raise his physical body from the grave, but instead appeared in a spiritual, subtle, or visionary body to the inward eye of his disciples, both individually and collectively? What difference would it make if these events occurred in an intermediate dimension, halfway between earth and what we call heaven? And the answer came: None. What matters is not a certain belief about Jesus or events presented in the Gospels but that the inner Christ is still rising in what Leonard Cohen calls "the caverns of the heart," and that people throughout history have had direct, personal experience of the mystical Christ.

Perhaps the post-resurrection appearances of Jesus, then, were indeed real – that is, direct visionary encounters with the ongoing presence of their departed Master. When poet and mystic William Blake says "visionary things are real," he means that they are not entirely subjective but also objective on another plane. If this is so, then the resurrection becomes not only the record of an experience of the disciples in ancient times but an ongoing event that can happen to any of us now. My sense is that the *Christos* (or integral human being) is being formed in each of us inwardly.

Keeping It Open

In light of the need to contextualize biblical narratives according to what we deem likely or possible, there is for me one caveat. It is wise to maintain an attitude of openness to the possibility of the mysterious or numinous. Some biblical scholars dismiss as improbable anything recorded in scripture that cannot pass through the sieve of empiricism. Yet when we apply this post-Cartesian measuring rod to mystical experience we eliminate a lot. I prefer to walk the ledge that affirms both immanence and transcendence. The divine emerges from a unified and inclusive realm beyond our current knowing, whether we call it within or beyond or above. For after all, these words are spatial metaphors for mystery.

I have discovered that Roman Catholicism and Eastern Orthodoxy have generally tolerated a greater openness to the miraculous than Protestantism, except in Protestantism's more charismatic forms. Pentecostals and evangelicals, for example, tend to be more open to the supernatural than liberal Protestants, partly because they are more comfortable with the literal interpretation of scripture. Yet they often stop at the literal and fail to understand that some narratives are clearly only symbolic or mythic.

Apparently supernatural occurrences like the Mary sightings at Lourdes, Fatima, and Medjugorje have been studied by medical doctors, psychologists, and theologians within the Catholic Church for both pathology and authenticity but are generally dismissed as superstition by Protestants. A fascinating book called *The Miracle Detective* by journalist Randall Sullivan explores the question of the authenticity of some such experiences. Sullivan's interviews with the Medjugorje mystics became a catalyst to his own mystical journey, and in the book he traces his move from skeptic to open-minded seeker. His investigations of the six young seers in war-torn Bosnia led him to rule out the possibility of them being fraudulent, delusional, or mad. On reading his account, I began to think that perhaps these experiences of Mother Mary in Medjugorje are modern manifestations of the universal feminine power of Sophia (divine Wisdom) operative through a group of fairly ordinary children. Perhaps these young people's experiences are genuine encounters with transcendent reality clothed in the accoutrements of their Catholic culture and tradition.

It is possible that certain archetypes emerge from a more inclusive dimension and are experienced at an intermediate plane of perception, where the knowing is not merely subjective or objective but transcends this distinction. Some of these experiences originate from the supraconscious level. The insistence on the either-or, subjective versus objective dynamic is part of a Western mindset that keeps us from opening to what French scholar Henry Corbin calls the intermediate or "imaginal" world, as distinguished from the purely imaginary or made-up. This imaginal world is the subtle realm of the angelic, between temporal reality and the ultimate divine Unity.

Close Encounters of the Visionary Kind

The reason I am fascinated with these sorts of speculations is because I have at various times in my life experienced things that seem unaccountable and can't be rejected as mere psychological projections: visionary dreams that surpass ordinary dreams so much that daily reality seems shadow-like in comparison. Some of these experiences I have kept to myself. Yet now, as I approach my mid-sixties, I feel free to share a few of them, the likes of which I suspect are more common than generally assumed.

When I was in my early twenties, I had an intense visionary experience of being on a pilgrimage. I was freed from a prison and joined a group of others in a grove of trees where the Christ manifested in unspeakably gold-white luminescence. As I reached to touch the edge of his aura, the voltage from his spiritual body pulsed through mine like a million megawatts of electricity and catapulted me out of the vision, where I found myself shouting, "He's real! He's real!" I didn't simply mean that I was convinced that the Christ existed, but that I had had a living encounter with the cosmic Christ who had before been essentially a figure of my belief system.

Another time, a few years later, in full waking consciousness, the image of the resurrected Christ manifested in a windowpane, becoming a living cross but without nail marks or other signs of the crucifixion. After this "showing," as Julian of Norwich called such visual images, an inner voice reverberated throughout the room saying, "If you go down with me you die with me; but when you descend with me, you rise up with me to everlasting life."

I was so shaken afterwards I could barely walk, and remained in an altered state for several days. At first I thought the vision might be a sign of my literal and imminent death or the onset of madness. After much reflection, I realized the message was that the core of me was eternal and deathless, but I had to resign my limited sense of self. In simpler terms, it was the same as Jesus' words to Nicodemus about being born again (but not "born again" in the sense used by many fundamentalists).

Some of these experiences have yielded deeper meaning in retrospect. For instance, a few years ago, some unexpected words emerged during prayer that seemed to complete the old dream of moving toward the radiant Christ: "You are the light you have been moving towards." These words imply that the figure of the luminous Christ in the early dream represented a state of consciousness that is within me already and of which I am mostly unaware – the Christ consciousness. Just in case you think I need an ego management workshop or an out-of-the-ego experience, I need to add that this recognition is not only universal but common in the mystical tradition. That is, mystics often speak of enlightenment as an awakening to what is always there within them.

It is not that we are gods, or equal to the Creator, but that divine Spirit indwells us. The infinite in us can meet the infinite in the love of the all-encompassing Mystery. As Olga Park put it of Jesus, "God was in the all of him, but he was not the all of God." God is in us too, but we are not the all of God.

The Cringe Factor over Woo-Wooism

People back off from the mystical partly out of fear, and sometimes rightly so. How does one distinguish, for instance, authentic visionary experience from delusions and pathological states? I am particularly sensitive to this question because there has been a history of schizophrenia in my immediate family and I'm quite apt to discredit such things as the hearing of voices. I would suggest that great visionaries and mystics such as William Blake, Teresa of Avila, and John of the Cross have already explored this question and laid out solid guidelines for those who inadvertently or intentionally find themselves on a mystical path. Garnering wisdom from here and there, I have put together a concise compendium for discernment of spirits, as reiterated by the major mystics.

- The underlying principle is that if we make mystical experience the end-point of our quest or attribute too great an importance to it, we have committed idolatry,[2] an old-fashioned term for substituting the ephemera or by-products for the end or purpose and becoming attached to what is secondary.
- It is never a good idea to try to induce mystical experience. However, if such an encounter comes upon us, we have to assess its value and authenticity and make an effort to interpret it and integrate it into our daily lives.
- Anything that aggrandizes the ego is immediately suspect. The ground rule for spiritual growth in all traditions is humility.
- It is important to seek balance and moderation in all things. Anyone who practices extreme spiritual disciplines can be in danger of leaving out the needs of the emotions, rational mind, and body.
- Divine revelations positively discourage self-righteous judgment (as opposed to spiritual discernment), them-us thinking, and the demonizing of others.
- Spiritual development increases the capacity to love ourselves and each other.

- Mystical experience bears fruits in our lives and manifests as goodness, justice, kindness, mercy, and compassion.
- Intimations of the mystical do not remove us from the world but enable us to engage with the world with increased dedication and hopefulness. Mystics are generally activists as well as contemplatives.
- Mystical awareness should not be used to make predictions about the future or to induce fear. We should never use mystical awareness as a means to control others.
- Anyone who has a numinous experience shouldn't assume he or she is better or more advanced than anyone who hasn't.

I still believe that these sorts of experiences – visionary dreams, hearing interior words of wisdom and consolation, encounters with loved ones who have passed – are part of our common humanity, and that we all have the potential for them. Many of us dismiss or repress such phenomena, or immerse ourselves in ordinary time in order to forget them because they demand something of us, some kind of inner growth.

Spiritual Supranaturalism

In quantum physics, matter behaves in strange ways, particles appear and disappear, and reality is altered by the perspective of the perceiver. Matter and consciousness are interwoven in complicated ways that we do not understand. All we know is that things like spontaneous remission from disease do sometimes occur in response to prayer, as happened with a friend of mine who was cured overnight of the most severe form of multiple sclerosis at the same time her whole church was praying for her.

We cannot expect such miracles, count on them, or know why some people are healed while others are not, but we need not deny that they happen. In the end, I prefer to remain wisely agnostic rather than dismissive, not equating every paranormal experience with the divine, but neither subscribing to the "believing all things" school. One thing is certain: the creative mind that moves within the cosmos cannot be locked forever in our diminutive boxes.

---

1 Bruce Sanguin, blog, January 31, 2011, Holy Holons, Batman!
   http://ifdarwinprayed.com/tenet-1-post-3-holy-holons-batman/
2 Antoinette Voûte Roeder, poet, from email conversation, January 2008.

Chapter Thirteen

I Am

I am the light of the world. Whoever follows me will never walk in darkness but will have the light of life.

~ JOHN 8:12

I am the way, and the truth, and the life. No one comes to the Father except through me.

~ JOHN 14:6

*I am the light
shining upon all things.
I am the sum of everything
for everything has come forth from me,
and towards me everything unfolds.*

~ THE GOSPEL OF THOMAS, LOGION 77

Prayer of Opening to I Am

*I am body, soul, and spirit,
and I am that I Am
that builds this body
and is me and not me
in the beginning
    that is still beginning*

*so I honour this body
from which I Am is
never separate
until I consign
my solar system of cells
    and nerves into the sea*

*from which I Am
comes again making
me and all that is
over and over new
from a mind-mine
    of endless surprise.*

*When the little self
that has served me so well
slumbers and sleeps
the great I Am opens its eye,
casting its nameless name
      into the world.*

*I am silent, humble,
unimposing to the outer eye,
but effective in thought and speech,
atomic in compassion,
claiming nothing for myself
      out of this everything I AM.*

When I was a kid in Sunday school, the *I Am* sayings of Jesus in the Gospel of John were presented as evidence that Jesus was both the only begotten son of God and the masculine God incarnate. No one seemed to see any contradiction between these two interpretations of Jesus' identity. It was clear Jesus was in a pretty special, even trans-human, category from birth; for anyone else to appropriate such sayings for him- or herself would be blasphemy. Lately, however, I have been wondering how we might take another look at the *I Am* sayings of Jesus so as to embed them in our lives today.

The *I Am* Sayings Revisited

Some of the more liberal biblical scholars have argued that the *I Am* sayings weren't likely spoken by Jesus at all, since no Jew would equate himself with the unspeakable Holy One of Israel. Jesus' assertion, "Before Abraham was, I Am," would have sounded shockingly blasphemous to Jewish ears, since he seems to be appropriating the unpronounceable name by which God revealed himself to Moses. Such statements likely moved the early Gentile Christian communities further and further away theologically from those of their Jewish Christian brothers and sisters. The Ebionites, or Jewish Christians of the first century who were centred in and near Jerusalem, for example, would have taken them as a challenge to their monotheism.

Another way of looking at the *I Am* sayings, whether or not spoken by Jesus, is to see that they show how the early Christian communities saw their teacher after his death. Jesus represented what God would look like if he came in human form.

Whatever the case, these passages were instrumental in providing the basis for later doctrines about Jesus as God that became part and parcel of orthodox teaching. The doctrine of the Trinity, where the Son is co-equal, co-eternal, and of one substance with the Father, emerged at the end of the fourth century, partly to resolve the conundrum of how Jesus as the Christ could be both fully human and fully divine.

What is not often emphasized, except among the mystical theologians, is that Jesus may have been teaching that each one of us is both fully human and fully divine. If we are all made in the image of God, as Genesis implies, then we are all in a sense potential incarnations of the *I Am*, chips off the old star block, divine scintillations. While our temporal selves may be partially identified with civilization's corrupt power systems, Jesus may be trying to point out that our centre of Being is essentially pure.

Thomas Merton calls this core where we are one with God, the *point vierge* or "virginal centre" that cannot be defiled by anything.[1] There is a holy spark informing our socially constructed selves that has never left the original unity. This *I Am* dwells in us and we dwell in the *I Am*.

John and Thomas

The first-century non-canonical Gospel of Thomas, rediscovered in Upper Egypt in 1945, draws out a similar insight about what Merton calls our "hidden wholeness." Here, Thomas, rather than Simon Peter, is depicted as the disciple who first recognizes who Jesus is. Yet rather than providing a term like Messiah or prophet or Son of God to describe his teacher, he acknowledges in him a mystery beyond naming.

> Thomas said:
> "Master, I cannot find words to express
> who you really are."
>
> Yeshua said,
> "Thomas, it is no longer necessary
> for me to be your Master

for you are drinking from the gushing
spring I have opened for you,
and you have come intoxicated."[2]

Thomas is not presented here as the doubter who fails to believe in Jesus till he sees the marks of the nails in his hands and feet, but as the disciple who first "gets it" that Jesus isn't simply making extravagant claims about himself. On the contrary, Jesus tries to help the disciples realize that they too can become bearers of the *I Am* consciousness.

Jesus says this eternal awareness is like being intoxicated in order to symbolize how each of us can access the ecstatic overflow of Spirit for him- or herself. He doesn't intend his learners to remain in kindergarten forever, but to mature into the spiritual life as his brothers, sisters, and friends. John implies the same when he has Jesus say on the night of the Last Supper, "I do not call you servants any longer…but I have called you friends" (John 15:15). Thomas' name, meaning "the twin," suggests the disciple's oneness with Jesus and the idea that each of us can become a twin or mirror of the Christ.

In the passage from Thomas at the beginning of this chapter, Jesus speaks as the "light shining on all things," "the sum of everything," and that from which everything comes. Here is the cosmic *I Am* speaking as the Alpha and

Omega, the divine source of all things, the power behind and within the manifest world. This speaking is not of the past but of the now, where creation is an ongoing process. The voice goes on to say,

> Split a piece of wood,
> and there I am.
> Pick up a stone
> and you will find me there.

For me, the passage implies that everything is alive and holy, even things we think of as inanimate, such as a piece of wood or a stone. Spirit is the source and underlying reality of everything, including me and you, wood, stones, fish, flowers, and birds. We are truly bathed in the *I Am* life forces all the time if we just lift up the apparently ordinary stones around us and look. Spirit is omnipresent in matter if we have eyes to see and ears to hear.

John's Mystical Mediator, *Logos-Sophia*

Scholar Elaine Pagels' book *Beyond Belief: the Secret Gospel of Thomas* argues that the Gospel of Thomas was written to counter the Gospel of John, and that the two accounts represent viewpoints of early rival Christian communities.[3] John emphasizes Jesus' divinity while Thomas explores the potential within us to become like Jesus. While Pagels may be correct about John and Thomas offering contending interpretations of Jesus' life and teachings, it seems to me the *I Am* sayings in John are as deeply mystical as in Thomas. John identifies Jesus as the *Logos* or mediating power in all things when he writes, "In the beginning was the Word, and the Word was with God, and the Word was God." John intentionally links the *Logos* or divine Word with divine feminine Wisdom or *Sophia* of the Hebrew tradition who was present with God from the beginning of the world. Jesus as the Christ is for John the child of Sophia, her incarnation in the world.

What, then, if we were actually part of this *Logos-Sophia* energy in the beginning? What if John can be read to be saying that everyone can go within to access the source of his or her own being?

The Universality of the *I Am* Sayings

Before moving to the question of what Jesus' *I Am* statements could mean to us now, I'd like to point out that such sayings are universal and can be found in the early poetry of many cultures. The sixth-century Welsh bard Taliesin employs *I Am* sayings, speaking (much like Sophia in Proverbs 8) as one present from the beginning.

> Before men walked
> I was in these places.
> I was here
> When the mountains were laid.
>
> I am as light
> To eyes long blind,
> I the stone
> Upon every grave.[4]

Such aphorisms are also common in ancient Egyptian poetry, which influenced the Jewish and Christian traditions. When we hear *I Am* sayings in ancient myth we are reminded of a level of reality that transcends the linear mindset of rationalism cut off from higher reason. We are lifted up collectively into the heart-wisdom of human awareness expressing itself from the perspective of timelessness.

Reinterpreting the *I Am* Sayings for Now

What if Jesus did use *I Am* sayings, but in a different context than has been assumed by most interpreters of the canonical gospels? What if he was not making special claims for himself, but calling forth the *I Am* or eternal consciousness hidden in each of us? For example, let's return to that famous saying, "I am the way, the truth, and the life. No one comes to the Father except through me." What if the gist of the passage is that the *I Am* consciousness in each of us is the Way or means to truth and light and that we can't access this universal, integral awareness except by affirming the eternal consciousness that already lies deep within us? We too are *I Am*.

What Is the *I Am* Consciousness?

One of the perennial questions asked by humankind is, Who am I? During my meditation practice once I asked, What is this *I Am* consciousness? And a response arose immediately: It is the eternal, the infinite love and compassion within you and within all living beings and things. So my prayer for the day became, Help me hook up to that within me that surpasses me. I began to realize that the *I Am* consciousness is completely immanent (or within) and completely transcendent (beyond my present knowing). So we all have the way, the truth, and the life within us but are not aware of it. It lies completely beyond the ego level as pure awareness. The ego, which is important as a building block in our development, is included in *I Am* but eventually must be swallowed up and transformed.

If the ego tries to appropriate the divine *I Am* on its own terms, we become egomaniacs, tyrants, or crazies. How many despots have crossed this line historically, equating their political or military power with God's agency or divine will? In fact, the ego must disappear in order for the *I Am* within us to appear. I contend that Jesus was not a crazy or an egomaniac, and that when he spoke to his disciples about the *I Am* within he was not claiming he was God except as everyone is potentially a repetition of the eternal I Am. After all, Jesus says in another context in John (quoting Psalm 82), "You are gods" (John 10:34).

Co-Creating with I Am in a Global Culture

Some people complain that they didn't choose to be here. "I didn't ask to be born," they grumble. Yet many of the mystics have hinted that we actually do so choose and that we co-create our bodies in the womb in cooperation with our mothers, God, and the angels. It has long amazed me that when I was in the womb, my cells knew exactly how to divide and form organs and the delicate instruments of the eye and inner ear, and that all this happened quite unconsciously. So if I could participate in the building of my amazing body when in a state of relative unconsciousness, what can the *I Am* in me do in a state of fully awakened consciousness?

The same principle applies to the collective. If we humans evolved unconsciously over millennia out of the earth, what might we as a species do collectively in a state of awakened consciousness? Perhaps this is the social-political implication of Jesus' *I Am* sayings. Awakened humanity can rebuild human community and find right relationship with the earth. It can make reparation to the other-than-human species. Collectively we have passed and are passing through the valley of the shadow of death – the wars, genocides, holocausts, and species extinctions of history. What lies on the other side of our collective shadow we do not yet know, but perhaps in the midst of crisis we can move to a more kind and compassionate way of being to enact Jesus' great dream: the kingdom of heaven on the earth.

The *I Am* sayings may just suggest that we are capable of co-creating with the powers within us to rescue the planet and ourselves through mutuality, cooperation, and a relinquishment of self-centred, us-them thinking. This is possible because the *I Am* in each of us is not an assertion of ego but a fountain of creativity that does not perceive anything as separate or outside itself to be left out, demonized, or made other.

We Too Are the Way, the Truth, and the Life

We are free to reinterpret the *I Am* sayings and reclaim them for our time. Certainly they don't apply exclusively to Jesus, for it was his intent to awaken deeper awareness in his learners, not set himself above them. People have variously approached the source of all being as the transcendent You or Thou and as the great network of being that is nature and the universe. Why not consider also approaching the power that moves things into harmony and balance as the great I Am, the very ground of our innermost being? Then we can say with Jesus, "I too am the light of the world. The words that I speak, they are Spirit and they are Life."

1 Thomas Merton, *Conjectures of a Guilty Bystander* (New York: Doubleday, 1968). "At the center of our being is a point of nothingness which is untouched by sin and by illusion, a point of pure truth, a point or spark which belongs entirely to God, which is never at our disposal....This little point of nothingness and of absolute poverty is the pure glory of God in us....It is like a pure diamond, blazing with the invisible light of heaven. It is in everybody...." (158).

2 "Logion 13," in *The Gospel of Thomas: Wisdom of the Twin.* (Trans. Lynn Bauman; Ashland, Oregon: White Cloud Press, 2004), 31.

3 Elaine Pagels, *Beyond Belief: the Secret Gospel of Thomas* (New York: Random House, 2003).

4 "Taliesin and the Mockers," in *The Collected Poems of Vernon Watkins* (Ipswich, Suffolk: Golgonooza Press, 1986), 318.

Chapter Fourteen

Re-visioning Revelation

And I saw the holy city, the New Jerusalem, coming down out of heaven from God, prepared as a bride adorned for her husband.

~ *REVELATION 21:2*

Unveiler of Mysteries,
Draw back the curtain that conceals and reveals
our most hidden, disarmed hearts.

Show us the flaming Christ we will become.
Show us the Anti-Christ, our lesser self who
*   must die.*

Open us to the Judgment that is transformation.
Open us to the Heavenly Jerusalem,
*   our capacity for peace.*

Help us build New Jerusalems in our
*   aching cities —*
cities clad in rags and jewels, sparkle and despair.

Wipe away the tears from all eyes
so we can inscribe our praises on our city walls.

Mainline liberal Christianity has steered clear of apocalyptic narratives like the book of Revelation and the prophetic visions of Daniel and Ezekiel. Some people think these wild dramatic-action sequences disclosing the "last things" or the end of time are so fraught with violence, dualism, good versus evil, them-us thinking, and rejection of this world that they are pretty much irrelevant in postmodern times and positively destructive to a progressive spiritual vision.

Despite the caveats of the historians, I am engaging unapologetically in the ancient Jewish interpretive tradition of *midrash,* or a symbolic interpretation of an earlier work. Midrash is an imaginative form of exegesis that goes beyond what the text might have meant exclusively in its historical context to find hints of its deeper meaning. Reading the imagery of Revelation as mystical symbolism enables us to reclaim much of its positive value.

Prophetic Speaking

First of all, the word prophet, meaning one who "speaks before," not only implies one who sees into the future but also one who sees deeply into the potential within the present. And the word apocalypse, when interpreted spiritually (symbolically), discloses a clash of powers within the human psyche mirrored over and over in the social-political spheres.

Certainly we need some understanding of mystical symbols in order to interpret John's puzzling visions in Revelation and reveal their transforming power. By a shifting of the frame, apocalypse can be read as a map of the evolution toward global consciousness and a new way of being on the earth. The imagery associated with the New Jerusalem may sound utopian, but apocalypse is by nature utopian in that its purpose is to help us imagine alternative realities.

Endings and Openings

Even the teachings of Jesus are strewn with eschatological or "end times" imagery. For instance, consider Jesus' prophecies of "those days" of tribulation when "the sun will be darkened, and the moon will not give its light" (Mark 13:24). Some scholars don't think Jesus said these things at all, but that they were interpretations by the gospel writers or editors. Other liberal biblical historians have placed many of these apocalyptic sayings in context as responses to Roman imperialism. They point out that apocalypse (meaning an "unveiling") is almost always produced during periods of oppression and represents the utopian hopes and dreams of the oppressed.

In John's revelation, the apocalyptic reversal occurs at the end of the age when the Christ overthrows the oppressive Roman system and the world is ruled by the formerly disempowered. According to the historian Eusebius, John, a leader in the new Christian movement, received the vision in about 95 CE during the reign of the emperor Domitian while he was imprisoned on the island of Patmos for "the testimony of Jesus Christ."

In the unfolding of the visions, the forces of the Christ overcome those of the anti-Christ. In the end, Rome co-opted Christianity by making it the official religion, and history plodded on with its succession of "wars and rumours of war." So using Revelation to predict doomsday for one's political oppressors flattens its rich and dramatic mystical symbolism.

William Blake, rather than rejecting apocalypse, delved into its symbolism to rewrite it as a story of our collective regeneration. He, like John, enacts a psychodrama of the divided soul where the various warring faculties of human consciousness are restored to order. If we stop insisting on using apocalypse to make dire predictions about the future or to justify resistance to whomever we consider our current enemy, the book might look quite different.

Numinous Archetypes

What if we took a few of the narrative's central symbols and examined them as archetypes? The first powerful image that blasts the seer John's psyche, after he hears the voice of the one he calls Alpha and Omega, is that of the burning Christ standing among the seven-branched candelabra:

> ....one like the Son of Man, clothed with a long robe and with a golden sash across his chest. His head and his hair were white as white wool, white as snow; his eyes were like a flame of fire, his feet were like burnished bronze, refined as in a furnace, and his voice was like the sound of many waters. In his right hand he held seven stars, and from his mouth came a sharp, two-edged sword, and his face was like the sun shining with full force.
>
> ~ REVELATION 1:13–16

This sublime figure is not simply a masculine-warrior version of Israel's Ancient of Days, but the Son of Man, or offspring of humanity. The voice of many waters represents the unification of the voices and visions of many peoples and nations into a harmonious whole. We can consider this as a figure of the beginning and the ending of human evolution, both its origin and end, or purpose. This luminous one represents humanity realized, evolved, "perfected" (fulfilled and whole).

The two-edged sword in his mouth is not a literal emblem of warfare but the divine Word of power, the right use of words and or language. The seven-branched Jewish menorah is John's symbol for seven channels, chakras, or energy centres of creative expression. The number seven in his numerology represents completion or wholeness. This glorious figure, then, is not what we are, but what we have the potential to be.

As the narrative proceeds, the polar opposite of this figure of light – the horrific anti-Christ – emerges to do battle with the saints, or those on the path to wholeness. In every era, human conquerors and dictators with an insatiable lust for power have been nominated for the role of anti-Christ, from Nero to Napoleon, Hitler to George Bush. Yet we are further along the road of poetic and symbolic thinking if we see this "rough Beast" as a mentality or a mindset rather than an individual.

One way of looking at the anti-Christ is that it represents that which is so firmly attached to the self-centred orientation that it destroys its own humanity in the course of trying to satisfy its greed and lust for power. The anti-Christ's illusion of autonomy threatens the well-being of all. It is systemic evil, that which drives wars, the dehumanization of society, the machinery of torture, and the exploitation of innocence. It is not a single human being, but an attraction within humanity to what psychologist James Hillman calls "the terrible love of war." It is inherently inhumane, or perhaps the all-too-human norm, a fear-based denial of the impulse toward compassion and peace-making that is our deeper inheritance. It is a counter-force to the trajectory of spiritual evolution. Yet this tendency is in each of us.

Reading Revelation is somewhat like gazing at the full spectrum of humanity, the best and the worst humans can be. It is to realize that we all bear in ourselves marks of both the Beast and the Lamb and that none of us is immune from this struggle over the best use of our considerable but limited powers.

Beastly Bedfellows

Scholars have pondered the meaning of the number 666 associated with the Beast. The best explanation I have heard yet was one provided by my mystic friend Olga Park, who suggested that the repeating sequence of sixes represents mankind's being stuck, so to speak, at level six, or willfully refusing to advance to level seven. Level six represents the mindset that no spiritual powers exist beyond those of human reason. Level seven represents the fully integrated Christ consciousness.

That the anti-Christ is initially bound and thrown into a pit but rises again, to be finally cast into a lake of fire by the Christ figure on a white horse, is a hint that true peace cannot be attained by a mere suppression of what we define as evil. These darker forces within us keep arising till they are radically transformed. The throwing of the beast into the "lake of fire" (Revelation 19:20) can be seen as something like an alchemical transmutation.

Luminous Lambs

Another striking symbol from the apocalypse of John is the Lamb of God. Certainly, this symbol needs to be lifted out of atonement theology, which holds the belief that God can't forgive people without a blood sacrifice. Though lambs were still sacrificed at the temple at the time of Jesus, Jesus did not teach an atonement theology or present his death as necessary for the forgiveness of sins.

What if we do not read this old sin-redemption theology into the text? What is most astonishing about the Lamb is the notion of such a humble creature being invested with the dignity of authority. The investiture of the lamb on the throne and its being given the scroll of the ages to open reinforces Jesus' teaching that the greatest among us is the one who serves. Rather than a mere inversion of oppressor and oppressed, however, the figure represents a reversal of our ordinary expectations of how socio-political systems work. Here we are shown a world where humility is power. In the big scheme of things, love and non-violence are surpassingly greater than pride and violence. The Lamb does not step up to the throne as victim. The image reveals that spiritual evolution can be furthered through the powers of gentleness and peacemaking, rather than might.

Shining Icons

What else shifts if we continue along this line of analysis? The communion of saints stands for a community where peace and justice replace our current survival-of-the-fittest economics. The marriage of the Bride and the Bridegroom is a shining icon for the male and female principles acting in harmony. The Woman Clothed in the Sun who is driven into the desert and given the wings of an eagle is not merely Israel or the Christian church, but the exiled divine feminine, Sophia, or cosmic Wisdom. She is hidden at the margins of the world being readied to give birth to the Christ-consciousness within humanity. And Babylon is not just Rome, but the corrupt power systems and empires of all ages.

The triumphant warrior on the white horse is not just a conquering hero like Achilles or Ajax, but an image of spiritual warfare against our primal aggressiveness. Moderate Muslims have pointed out that the word *jihad* has been co-opted by fundamentalist factions within Islam to represent physical warfare, but that in its truest sense it means spiritual warfare. The Battle of Armageddon, whose mere name is the stuff of big budget disaster films, is the final showdown between the part of humanity acting out of the old reptilian fight-or-flight brain and the new consciousness that creates positive change through cooperation.

The throne of God around which the four Cherubim gather becomes the seat of divine manifestation, the centre from which the world constantly emanates – the very seat of creative energy. The Last Judgment is an ultimate freeing of human consciousness from the urge to treat others as anything other than ourselves.

Justice, Not Punitive Judgment

Often, all people remember about the book of Revelation is the fire and brimstone cast from heaven as chastisements as the seven seals are opened. What if we view this scenario instead as a symbol of the natural consequences that come into play through humanity's abuse of the earth and of each other? The triumphant ending of the apocalypse suggests strongly that is possible for humans, in cooperation with Spirit, to turn things around by abandoning systems that are not working while releasing our latent collective creativity.

Peace and the City

The descent of the New Jerusalem from above, the marriage of heaven and earth, represents the union of spirit and matter, the transcendent and the immanent, and is a vision for living in balance with the planet.

> Then I saw a new heaven and a new earth; for the first heaven and the first earth had passed away, and the sea was no more. And I saw the holy city, the new Jerusalem, coming down out of heaven from

God, prepared as a bride adorned for her husband.
And I heard a loud voice from the throne saying,
"See, the home of God is among mortals.
He will dwell with them;
they will be his peoples,
and God himself will be with them;
he will wipe every tear from their eyes.
Death will be no more;
mourning and crying and pain will be no more,
for the first things have passed away."

~ *REVELATION 21:1–4*

Again, if we take the images literally, we are forced to imagine a world without an ocean, or one of static perfection. However, in this context the sea represents the destructive forces of social chaos. To say there is no more sea may indicate that the destructive, chaotic elements of consciousness have been raised to a spiritual level. The voice announcing that God is among us is similar to Paul's teaching that humans are the temples or sacred tabernacles of God. God is no longer perceived as lofty, remote, and other, but as the radiant ground of being in the innermost self and in all things.

The expulsion of death means that death will be experienced as the transformation or the falling away of the old self. The poignant image of God wiping away our tears is one that is often forgotten when people think of the figure of God in the Apocalypse. Here the Holy One of Israel is a compassionate and intimate friend.

The translucent image of the New Jerusalem as a twelve-gated community resting on twelve foundation stones made of various precious stones is rooted in Israel's prophetic tradition. There is a similar symbolism (jewels on the breastplate of the high priest) in Ezekiel, and this imagery was carried forward into Christianity. The twelve tribes of Israel, for instance, become the twelve Apostles or founders of Christianity. The breathtaking image of heaven as a city of shining jewels and light has entered popular mythology.

Unfortunately, the image of communal humanity as a divine city is sometimes associated with a static or cold heaven where everything is "too perfect" and there is no room for growth. I would urge that perfection in this context is dynamic, and the dazzling colours of the jewels represent various aspects of consciousness that shine out when humans abandon their brutality.

Jerusalem, Now

Contrary to common assumptions, the Apocalypse is a visionary work of outrageous hopefulness. It reveals a possible future where humans live justly and in harmony with each other and the earth. The vision isn't deterministic, however, as it doesn't override our individual and collective exercise of free will. It depicts a thrust toward wholeness – psychological, political, and cultural – in which we are invited to participate. It's an invitation for us to be co-creators in an emerging order, the "new heaven and the new earth" that could be a reality in the present, not just the hereafter.

I'd like to propose a final possibility. If one looks at history as a train riding along rails, or anything that goes in a line from point A to point B, it's hard to see consistent evidence of evolutionary progress in human history. In fact, we seem to be devolving as much as we are evolving. And maybe we are doing both.

The 20th century has been an era of massive warfare and genocide, as well as one of amazing technological advances. Yet if one thinks of evolution not as linear, but as an upward spiral with its own torque of grace, there are signs of a hidden movement toward cooperation as the only means of survival. Revelation, then, is not simply the story of emergent human consciousness but the simultaneous descent of Spirit into matter to create a new sphere of life, "a new heaven and a new earth." In the unveiling of the New Jerusalem, transcendence (God beyond us) and immanence (God within us) converge. Spirit descends into matter while matter simultaneously rises into Spirit. Spirit becomes more substantial and substance more spiritual.

The image of the holy Jerusalem descending from heaven as a bride is the transcendent half of the equation. Spiritual evolution as heralded in John's apocalypse is not simply a movement towards mere improvement of what is and what has been, but a creation of something entirely new. John's prophetic vision is the book of Genesis retold: God's creation of a new earth with the cooperation of humanity and the angelic orders. The old serpent in the garden, grown to full size as the dragon, is cast out. Revelation, then, is a prophetic glimpse of what the world looks like when love sits on the throne of consciousness. It offers hope that we can still transform our humanitarian and environmental crises and live in harmony with each other and creation.

The potent imagery of the fall of Babylon and the destruction of destructive ways reveals that the New Jerusalem will not be won through warfare and enmity but through a painful process of inner and outer transformation. In the end, this apparent doomsday scenario can be read as one of the world's great peace poems. After all, Jerusalem means "city of Peace," but the peace presented is not merely the absence of war, avoidance of conflict, or "the [false] peace that will destroy many." It is the peace that "surpasses all understanding."

Acknowledgements

Earlier versions of the following chapters were published in *The United Church Observer*: "The Paradise Ear," October 2006; "Transforming the Shadow," June 2007; and "The Problem with Perfect," June 2008. The latter won a Canadian Church Press Award for 2009.

An earlier version of "Countering War with Wonder" appeared in *The Pacific Rim Review of Books*. Issue 8 (Spring 2008), 35–37.

"Rapturous Ravishments in the Song of Songs" was published in *Room: a Space of Your Own*. Issue 33.4: All of Us Sacred (Winter 2011).

Some chapters were delivered first as lay sermons at Canadian Memorial United Church in Vancouver, British Columbia.

"The Paradise Ear," May 28, 2006. http://www.canadianmemorial.org/Sermons/printer/2006May28.pdf

"Transforming the Shadow," March 4, 2007. http://www.canadianmemorial.org/Sermons/printer/2007Mar04.pdf

"The Problem with Perfect," as "Repositioning Perfection" Nov. 18, 2007. http://www.canadianmemorial.org/Sermons/printer/2007Nov18.pdf

"Rapturous Ravishments" as "Rapturous Ravishments in the Song of Songs," Feb. 3, 2007. http://www.canadianmemorial.org/Sermons/2008%2002_03.htm

"Peaceful Resisters," June 15, 2008. http://www.canadianmemorial.org/sermons.htm

"Fire on Fire," May 31, 2009. http://www.canadianmemorial.org/sermons_2/2009_11_08.html

"A Warless World," Nov. 8, 2009. http://www.canadianmemorial.org/sermons_2/2009_05_31.html

"The Palace of Presence," May 22, 2010. http://www.canadianmemorial.org/sermons_2/2010_08_22.html

"I Am," April 3, 2011. http://www.canadianmemorial.org/sermons/545-sermon-20110403-i-am-by-susan-mccalin

I would like to acknowledge the original publishers of my poems cited in this book:
At the Mercy Seat. Vancouver, BC: Ronsdale Press, 2003.
A Plot of Light. Lantzville, BC: Oolichan Books, 2004.
Lifting the Stone. Toronto: Seraphim Editions, 2007.
Persephone Tours the Underground. North Vancouver, BC: Alfred Gustav Press, 2009.
Demeter Goes Skydiving. Edmonton, AB: University of Alberta Press, 2011.